Napoleon Hill's
Greatest
Speeches

Napoleon Hill's
Greatest
Speeches

From the Archives
Never Before Published Writings by
NAPOLEON HILL

SOUND WISDOM
P.O. Box 310
Shippensburg, PA 17257-0310

For more information on publishing and distribution rights, call 717-530-2122. International rights inquiries please contact The Napoleon Hill Foundation at 276-328-6700 or email NapoleonHill@uvawise.edu

Reach us on the Internet: www.soundwisdom.com.

ISBN 13 TP: 978-1-937879-80-8
ISBN 13 HC: 978-0-7684-1019-8
ISBN Ebook: 978-0-7684-1020-4

Cover Design by Eileen Rockwell
Interior Design by Terry Clifton

Publisher's Notes: Not all references to economy and conditions have been updated from original writing. We think you'll agree that the messages contained in this book are timeless.

While efforts have been made to verify information contained in this publication, neither the author nor the publisher assumes any responsibility for errors, inaccuracies, or omissions.

While this publication is chock-full of useful, practical information; it is not intended to be legal or accounting advice. All readers are advised to seek competent lawyers and accountants to follow laws and regulations that may apply to specific situations.

The reader of this publication assumes responsibility for the use of the information. The author and publisher assume no responsibility or liability whatsoever on the behalf of the reader of this publication.

For Worldwide Distribution, Printed in the U.S.A.
1 2 3 4 5 6 7 8 9 / 21 20 19 18 17

Library of Congress Cataloging-in-Publication Data
Names: Hill, Napoleon, 1883-1970, author.
Title: Napoleon Hill's greatest speeches / Napoleon Hill.
Description: Shippensburg, PA : Sound Wisdom, [2016] | Includes
bibliographical references.
Identifiers: LCCN 2016014113 | ISBN 9780768410198 (hardcover)
Subjects: LCSH: Success. | New Thought.
Classification: LCC BF637.S8 H486 2016 | DDC 650.1--dc23

LC record available at https://lccn.loc.gov/2016014113

Contents

Foreword

by
Dr. J. B. Hill

Napoleon Hill rarely used more than a single page of notes to deliver his speeches. While many of these notes still exist, little of what he actually said has survived. It took me many years to locate one of my grandfather's speeches in print. Finding one was more than just exhilarating to me; it was miraculous.

The document I found was a transcript of a commencement address that Napoleon gave at Salem College (now Salem International University) in 1922. It had been published in a local newspaper under the title "The End of the Rainbow." A copy was preserved on microfilm in the archives of Salem College. When printed, it required magnification to read, and the text was so faded that it took more than a day to recover, which I did by dictating it one word at a time to my wife.

Napoleon wrote many times that adversity should be viewed as a blessing in disguise. In the 1922 commencement address, Napoleon shows how his many business failures were actually turning points that led him to greater opportunities. Each failure had therefore been a blessing.

He attributes his success following failure to the habit of performing more and better service than he was being paid for. This trait was the precursor of two of his principles of success: *Learning from Adversity and Defeat* and *Going the Extra Mile.*

Napoleon delivered the 1922 speech in Salem, West Virginia, not far from his wife, Florence's family home in Lumberport. Although he was the editor and publisher of *Napoleon Hill's Magazine* at the time and a success by every measure, he had much to prove to family. Ten business failures in a dozen years had soured family attitudes toward him. So, the commencement address was Napoleon's opportunity to be applauded before his wife's friends and family, and in this, he succeeded. His delivery rhythm was mesmerizing to his audience. He used his personal history of failures to demonstrate how he was able to overcome adversity. The speech was touted to be the greatest ever given in that part of the state. When it ended, amid resounding applause, Napoleon stood before family, vindicated.

I sent a copy of the speech to Don Green, who is executive director of the Napoleon Hill Foundation. Don immediately saw the potential for a book and began searching through the archives of the foundation for additional material. Over several years, he discovered a few more speeches and a number of articles that he collated for this book.

One of the articles, "This Changing World," had been discovered behind the mantel of a fireplace in Napoleon's boyhood home. It was written during the Great Depression, probably near the end of 1930.

When the Depression struck, Napoleon was living with family who provided him with secure employment. However, to him, his acceptance of that security meant that he had failed. So, in March 1931, Hill did exactly what he needed to do—and perhaps exactly what he shouldn't have done: he quit his job and left for Washington, DC.

By this time, Napoleon's list of failed business ventures was impressive. His decision to try once more to succeed on his own must have been founded in faith—he certainly possessed little else. The article retrieved from behind the mantel provides an understanding of that faith and insight into why Napoleon later left family and security for Washington, DC, during a worldwide depression. "This Changing World" answers many persistent questions concerning Napoleon's spiritual views.

Don also located two copies of one of Napoleon's earliest speeches, "What I Learned from Analyzing Ten Thousand People." One had been stored in the Napoleon Hill Foundation archives, and the other had been published in the February 1918 issue of *Modern Methods*. Napoleon wrote the speech while serving as dean of the George Washington

Institute of Advertising (now the Bryant & Stratton Business College of Chicago), where he later became president and director of the Salesmanship and Advertising Department.

In this speech, Napoleon talks about the five "requisites" for success: self-confidence, enthusiasm, concentration, a working plan, and the habit of performing more and better services than paid for. It reveals Napoleon's early thinking about three of what would become some of his principles of success: *Enthusiasm, Controlled Attention,* and *Going the Extra Mile.* Later he grouped the requisite of "self-confidence" under the heading of *Enthusiasm,* and "a working plan" became part of the process of achieving a *Definite Major Purpose.* Although Napoleon understood the importance of Andrew Carnegie's "Master Mind" idea, he did not mention it in this speech. I suspect it just wasn't pertinent for an audience of salesmen who tend toward having individual pathways to success.

At the end of 1952, Napoleon left his wife, Annie Lou, in California for a year while he worked with W. Clement Stone on a number of projects. For several months he and Stone toured together on the lecture circuit, with Stone often introducing Napoleon as a keynote speaker.

Don discovered a recording of one of these keynotes titled "Maker of Miracle Men" and had it transcribed for this book. It is perhaps the most interesting of his finds because it faithfully depicts Napoleon in extemporaneous mode. Napoleon's wit and spellbinding oratory is palpable in the prose.

By the middle of the 1950s, Napoleon was well known nationally as a speaker. His lectures had spread to radio and television, and Pacific International University had awarded him an honorary doctor of literature degree. In 1957, Salem College invited him back to give a baccalaureate sermon and to receive a second honorary doctorate.

By this time, Napoleon's ideas about success had matured until they had morphed into concrete principles. Instead of lecturing about the five *requisites* for success, he covers in his baccalaureate sermon, titled "The Five Essentials of Success," the five most important *principles* of success. Like the 1922 commencement speech, it too was applauded wildly by his audience.

It is interesting to note that after thirty-five years of thought, only *Going the Extra Mile* among the original five 1922 requisites for success remained essential in Napoleon's mind. The other requisites had been replaced by four essential principles: *Master Mind, Definiteness of Purpose, Self-Discipline,* and *Applied Faith.*

While each of the speeches and articles in this collection stands alone, together they show how Napoleon's ideas evolved as his thought matured and coalesced into a comprehensive philosophy of success. The aggregated material truly has greater significance than its parts.

Introduction

by
Don M. Green

Napoleon Hill was born on October 26, 1883. On his birth certificate his name was given as Oliver Napoleon Hill, though he dropped the "Oliver" from his name before he became well known as a writer.

There was not much in Hill's initial environment that would have suggested the career path he would take in his lifetime. Wise County, Virginia, where he grew up, is a remote region in the Appalachian Mountains.

Hill's biography, *A Lifetime of Riches*, portrays life in Wise County in the 1880s as isolated from most of the progress that was happening in much of the country. Life expectancy was short, infant mortality was high, and tens of thousands of rural Virginians suffered from chronic health problems ranging from hookworm to malaria to pellagra, a disease caused by inadequate diet.

Most of the schools in Virginia in the 1880s were in terrible shape. Elementary schools were open about four months out of the year, and attendance was not required. There were fewer than one hundred high schools in the state of Virginia at the time, and most of the programs were only two or three years in length. There were just ten four-year high schools in the entire state.

At the time of Hill's birth, coal was used for heating, but it was not commercialized until the 1890s. Farming on the mostly rocky, hilly terrain of Southwest Virginia was difficult, and many families left the mountains and moved to cities in search of jobs that offered more livable wages.

Corn was the main crop. Grown to make food for both animals and humans, it was also often used to make a type of liquor known as moonshine. The importance of moonshine was that it could be translated into cash, a precious, scarce commodity to mountain inhabitants.

This background of Hill gave him ample reasons later in life to proclaim that mountain culture was famous for three things: feuds, moonshine, and uneducated people.

In the archives of the Napoleon Hill Foundation is an unpublished autobiography in which Hill wrote, "For three generations my people had been born, lived, struggled in ignorance, illiteracy, and poverty and died without having been outside the mountains of that section. They made their living from the soil. Whatever money they procured was from the sale of corn converted into moonshine.... There were no railroads, telephones, electric lights, or passable public highways."

Note: Quotes and true stories shared with you here have been gleaned from archives, memories, discussions, handwritten letters, and other credible sources stored with the Napoleon Hill Foundation.

No doubt Hill was similar to others who admired wealthy people such as Andrew Carnegie, probably the richest man to ever live, and Thomas Edison, who gave us the light bulb around the same time of Hill's birth. However, unlike the typical admirer of the rich and famous, Hill met most of the country's affluent and powerful men of the time.

Destined to become Famous

Hill was destined to become famous. Today, literally hundreds of his most famous quotes are referenced. One of the most well-known is "Behind every adversity is the seed of an equivalent benefit." This quote could surely be applied to Hill's early childhood.

Hill's father, James Monroe Hill, took a young bride, Sara Blair, when he himself was only seventeen years old. Oliver Napoleon was the firstborn child, and his younger brother was named Vivian. Hill's mother died when he was only nine years old.

While the loss of his mother at such an early age dealt him a large blow, a year later he was blessed with a stepmother. Martha Ramey Banner, the widow of a school principal and the daughter of a local physician, had a greater impact on Hill's life than perhaps anyone else. He would later remark—in a statement reminiscent of what President Abraham Lincoln supposedly said concerning his stepmother—that "all that I am or ever aspire to be I owe to that dear woman."

Martha brought her three children and the two Hill brothers together and set out to improve the spiritual as well as the financial conditions of the new family. Martha exerted a profound influence over the whole family, starting with James, her new husband. She encouraged him to open a new post office and start selling merchandise, and he also helped establish the Three Forks Primitive Baptist Church.

Becoming active in this church would no doubt have a bearing on Hill's future, for it was probably his first exposure to an environment where the preachers could excite and move a congregation with their oratorical skills. Hill eventually became well known for his ability to captivate and convince audiences.

At the age of eleven Hill was persuaded by his stepmother to consider becoming a writer because of his unbounded imagination. Martha said to her stepson, "If you would devote as much time to reading and writing as you have to causing trouble, you might live to see the time when your influence will be felt throughout the state."

By the time Hill was twelve, his stepmother had convinced him to trade the gun he was so proud of for a typewriter. This was in 1895, when typewriters were not readily available. Martha again encouraged the often mischievous boy, telling him, "If you become as good with a typewriter as you are with that gun, you may become rich and famous and known throughout the world." Hill had read a tremendous amount and had learned that great writers could achieve widespread fame that could even last beyond one's own lifetime.

Even at an early age, the young Hill had begun to realize that a seed of thought planted by his stepmother could take root and grow. Later in life he would popularize the phrase "Whatever the mind of man can conceive, it can achieve."

At the age of thirteen, Hill took a job as a laborer at a coal mine for wages of a dollar per day. Not only was the work hard, dirty, and menial, but Hill only netted fifty cents per day, the other fifty cents going for his room and board. Hill did not see a future in coal mining, but it taught him that he could accomplish more using his mind than he could using his hands.

At the age of fifteen, Hill entered the two-year Gladesville High School and finished the work, though it was often not easy for him.

After high school Hill left home to attend a business school where the one-year program included shorthand, typing, and bookkeeping, skills meant to prepare students for the job of secretary.

Upon completion of business school, the seventeen-year-old Hill approached Rufus Ayers, a well-known attorney who had served as Virginia's Attorney General, for a job. Ayers was truly a man of many talents, for he was not only an attorney, but he was also deeply involved in the lumber and coal industries. Hill contacted Ayers because he admired wealthy business tycoons and dreamed of joining their ranks in the future.

Hill wrote Ayers a letter that showed the seriousness of his wish to work for him. In this letter he offered the following proposition:

> I have just completed a business college course and am well qualified to serve as your secretary, a position I am very anxious to have. Because I have no previous experience, I know that at the beginning, working for you will be of more value to me than it will be to you. Because of this I am willing to pay for the privilege of working with you.
>
> You may charge any sum you consider fair, provided at the end of three months that amount will become my salary. The sum that I am to pay you can be deducted from what you pay me when I start to earn money.

Working for Ayers proved to be very satisfying to Hill. Napoleon dressed in an excellent fashion, arrived at the job early, and stayed late. Hill's efforts certainly paid off, and it is easy to see how going the extra mile benefitted the aspiring businessman early in his career.

Encouraged by Ayers, Hill began to see himself as a successful lawyer. He convinced his brother, Vivian, to apply to law school at Georgetown University, saying that he could support them both with his writing. While Napoleon also attended law school, he did not graduate as his younger brother did. One particular writing assignment Hill received would define his vocation for the rest of his life. In the fall of 1908, Hill was asked to interview the steel magnate Andrew Carnegie for *Bob Taylor's Magazine*, a periodical owned by Robert Taylor, who had been governor of Tennessee and a United States senator. The magazine appealed to Hill because it featured stories of successful individuals. He was excited to use his talents from the days he wrote articles for newspapers in his youth.

The Carnegie Interview

The interview with Carnegie would be revolutionary for the field of self-improvement. Carnegie himself was a Horatio Alger rags-to-riches story. As a young Scottish immigrant with very little schooling, Carnegie went to work at the age of ten for a little over a dollar a week. By applying himself, saving, and investing, he was a millionaire by the age of thirty.

During the interview, Carnegie discussed the idea of a "philosophy of success," challenging Hill to spend twenty years interviewing and studying successful people to make available this philosophy to others. Carnegie contributed to this project by providing letters of introduction, which made contact with the country's most successful people possible for the young writer.

Hill accepted the challenge with which Carnegie presented him during the three-day interview, using the time to start learning Carnegie's philosophy of success. In discussions of his boyhood, Carnegie emphasized the *Master*

Mind principle and the *Going the Extra Mile* principle and how they had aided his career.

Carnegie told Hill that humble origins were not a hindrance to success but just an inspiration to overcome adversity and attain seemingly impossible goals. With a strong sense of self-worth, Carnegie said, "No amount of poverty can keep one from success. Confidence is a state of mind, necessary to succeed, and the starting point of developing self-confidence is definiteness of purpose." Carnegie's cardinal rule in what he called his "philosophy of personal achievement" was the following: "The man who knows exactly what he wants, has a definite plan for getting it, and is actually engaged in carrying out his plan will soon believe he has the ability in himself to succeed. The man who procrastinates soon loses confidence and does little or nothing worthwhile."

Hill asked Carnegie, "What happens when a man knows what he wants, makes his plans, takes action and meets with failure? Does not that destroy his confidence?"

Carnegie replied, "Every failure carries within it the seed of an equivalent benefit. Great leaders' lives show that their success is in proportion to their mastery of temporary defeat."

Carnegie also explained to Hill the necessity of controlling one's own thoughts. The mind, Carnegie reasoned, is the source of all happiness and all misery, of both poverty and riches. The use of our minds allows us to create friends or enemies. It is our choice. The limitations on one's mind are those that one imposes on himself.

Hill alluded to Carnegie's ideas about the mind when he repeatedly spoke and wrote, "Whatever the mind can conceive and believe, the mind can achieve."

Carnegie related to Hill that his friends such as Henry Ford, Thomas Edison, John D. Rockefeller, Harvey Firestone, and Alexander Graham Bell led lives similar to his. By trial and error, with a definite purpose and resolute actions, they earned not only success, but also wealth and fame. According to Carnegie, action is of the utmost importance because without it, the best plans and purposes are worthless. With these examples, Carnegie inspired Hill to study the lives of other great men.

> *Action is of the utmost importance because without it, the best plans and purposes are worthless.*

Hill applied these lessons in his lifelong quest to spread the philosophy of success that he learned from Carnegie and hundreds of leaders in business and government. His conversation with Carnegie became the basis of *Think and Grow Rich*, the best-selling and most influential self-improvement book ever written.

Shortly after his marriage, while living in Washington, DC, Hill went to Detroit to interview Henry Ford. Ford demonstrated he had self-control and the ability to concentrate all his efforts on attaining his goal, which was to produce an automobile that could be afforded by the masses. Hill said later that instead of discussing success,

Ford wanted to talk about his car. It must have impressed Hill because he purchased a new Model T Ford at a cost of $680 and drove it on the trip back to Washington to surprise his wife, Florence.

After his trip to Detroit to interview Henry Ford, Hill then found himself in desperate need of money. Recently married, he required a steady income. The answer appeared to be working as a salesperson with an automobile company in Washington, DC. This new job gave Hill an opportunity to go the extra mile. Hill began to train other salespeople through the Automobile College of Washington that he founded.

Hill encountered many challenges in life, but he was not prepared for that which would come with the birth of his son, Napoleon Blair Hill, on November 11, 1912. Napoleon Blair was born not only deaf, but without any ears. Rather than get instructions on how to learn sign language, Napoleon Hill Sr. was determined to teach his son to speak and hear. Hill would talk to the young boy for hours at a time by placing his lips on the base of the boy's neck, behind where his ears should have been. Years later, Blair learned to hear, and he eventually obtained a special hearing aid that further improved his hearing and speaking.

Hill inspired his son's desire to overcome the physical impediment of being born without ears. Napoleon faced many other difficulties in his life, such as broken marriages, failed businesses, and lack of finances, but he never gave up on his pursuit of the philosophy of success.

One of the businesses Hill started was the George Washington Institute, established to teach salesmanship. His sales course endeavored to teach advertising and the principle of service to others. Hill said that by this point in his life, he had interviewed over ten thousand men and women who were trying to succeed. He taught that self-confidence and enthusiasm are necessary for salespeople to succeed. Around this time, Hill began applying psychology to his philosophy of success. In one typed lesson from 1916 he remarks, "I seriously doubt that such a thing is possible as failing to get what one really wants. The truth is you are either consciously or unconsciously getting that which you think about most intensely." During this period in Hill's teaching career he began instructing his students that "auto-suggestion" would help discipline the mind.

The ending of World War I meant a change of circumstances. Hill conceived the idea of his first magazine, which he called *Napoleon Hill's Golden Rule Magazine.* For the publisher, Hill chose George Williams, whom he had met while they both were working for President Woodrow Wilson during the war.

Working on *Napoleon Hill's Golden Rule Magazine,* Hill put to use his past experience with a typewriter and his prior knowledge of newspapers. The publication served as a great outlet for the enthusiasm he recalled from the Three Forks Primitive Baptist Church located on the Powell River in Wise County, Virginia. This was an opportunity for Hill to spread his message, to lecture, and to excite his audiences.

Here he was at last to achieve the fame his stepmother had promised him as a youth.

The first issue of *Napoleon Hill's Golden Rule Magazine* was written, edited, printed, and delivered to newsstands in January 1919. Due to the lack of funds to hire writers Hill wrote every word of the first nine issues. He later said, "I wrote every word and used pen names to cover my identity." With just one writer, *Napoleon Hill's Golden Rule Magazine* should not have been a success, but it was. The first issue sold so fast it was printed three times.

By October 1920 Hill had lost ownership of *Napoleon Hill's Golden Rule Magazine*. He then began traveling throughout the United States, giving speeches brimming with enthusiasm. He was well received wherever he went.

In 1921, after Hill had moved from Chicago to New York, he started *Napoleon Hill's Magazine* and published the first issue in April 1921. While Hill authored the majority of the pieces, he began to use other writers, who covered a broad array of subjects, including doctors, businessmen, and psychologists. Hill began to give advice on how to build self-confidence, how to sell one's self, and even how to get a better job.

Hill used the magazine to publicize his lectures to people involved in sales, advertising, and to civic organizations and colleges. All this activity was intended to promote his philosophy. Hill's lectures began to be in such demand that he was receiving fees of one hundred dollars plus extra money to cover his expenses.

Emotionally Charged Speeches

Napoleon was overjoyed with his public speaking career because it enabled him to see the effect of his teaching—indeed, his words and delivery moved audiences. His speeches were emotionally charged and often incorporated proverbs from the Bible that he no doubt remembered from the sermons of the Three Forks Primitive Baptist Church.

Hill concentrated primarily on two main topics, one being the Magic Ladder to Success, which happens to be the title of his second book, published in 1930. The other topic was the Golden Rule philosophy, which continued to guide his speaking and writing. Hill also spoke of the "seven turning points in his life." Hill's message was conveyed through stories of failures and successes taken from both his personal and professional life.

In 1921, while *Napoleon Hill's Magazine* was doing well, Hill started something new in the field of communications. Advertising through his lectures, he developed a course called the Science of Success, which the public could purchase by mail order. It included ten printed lessons and six phonograph records. The owner of the Science of Success course could read Hill and listen to his dynamic voice. This program was a forerunner of the audio motivational industry, which boasts a following of millions of enthusiasts devoted to improving their lives.

By 1922 Hill's lectures not only were commanding large fees, but they also were connecting him with rich and famous businesspeople while he continued to work on the philosophy of success that Carnegie had challenged him to develop.

But Hill was not satisfied with teaching the philosophy of success only to the general public; he saw the opportunity and need to teach his formula for success to the prison population as well.

Hill began teaching the philosophy in prison, and it was an immediate success. Today it continues to help prepare inmates for a better life. Tens of thousands of incarcerated people have benefited from the material Hill developed, often using it to gain a new start in their lives.

Having lost *Napoleon Hill's Golden Rule Magazine* to his partner and being later forced to abandon *Napoleon Hill's Magazine,* Hill had suffered some very costly business dealings. But nobody bounced back from adversity better than Hill, who serves as a prime example of the principle that "every adversity carries within it the seed of an equivalent or greater benefit."

Shortly thereafter, Hill used creative financing to purchase a building for $125,000 to start the Metropolitan Business College.

Once the business school was in full operation, Hill began in 1924 to lecture as frequently as three times a day, five days a week.

By 1926 Hill had met Don Mellett, publisher of the *Canton Daily News* in Canton, Ohio. Transferring management of his business school to his partner, he began full-time employment with the *Canton Daily News*. Mellett was so impressed with Hill that he wanted to put Hill's lifetime of studies and research on success into a book.

But Hill was to meet with yet another tragedy. It was the Prohibition era, and Mellett had exposed a group of sellers of illegal whiskey. A policeman-turned-gangster murdered Mellett. Hill—thought to have been involved in the exposé—had to flee to save his life. Hill was so close to seeing his first book published, but the murder of his partner temporarily put those plans on hold.

Hill was to be delayed but not denied. After staying in West Virginia, where his wife's relatives lived, he went to Philadelphia with the mission of getting his first book published. After receiving numerous rejections for the gigantic manuscript, Hill remembered the name of Andrew Pelton, an advertiser in *Napoleon Hill's Golden Rule Magazine*. Pelton reviewed Hill's work and quickly agreed to provide capital for the printing and distribution of his book, plus a large advance for Hill.

Hill dedicated twelve to eighteen hours a day to retyping and updating the huge manuscript. Just as when he had started to publish *Napoleon Hill's Golden Rule Magazine,* he not only typed every page of the tremendous volume himself, but he also served as the sole copy editor and proofreader. The result was a lively, passionate, and much-improved manuscript. The rewrite took three months, and Hill was so pleased with the end product that he described it to his wife as "one hundred percent better than before." It took an eight-volume series to cover Hill's work. Titled *The Law of Success*, it became the most complete work on success ever written.

The Law of Success

The eight-volume set originally cost over thirty dollars. Despite this being a large sum for the time, the series sold well. Hill received his first royalty checks from *The Law of Success* in 1928, and by early the next year they were averaging $2,500 per month, a tremendous income for 1929.

The Law of Success was initially rejected by publishers, but its acceptance by the public overwhelmed the many self-help books in the market at the time. Hill considered it to be more than a book; he viewed it as a set of instructions on how to get ahead in life. All the information Hill presented in *The Law of Success* resulted from Carnegie's instructions to conduct interviews and do research to obtain advice from America's most successful individuals. A law can be interpreted as rules, but as written by Hill, *The Law* was fact and testimony to the success of capitalism. No previously published piece of literature compared with *The Law of Success*.

With the profits from *The Law of Success* Hill was able to purchase a Rolls-Royce automobile in 1929 and a 680-acre estate in New York's Catskill Mountains. However, shortly thereafter Hill's fortune was consumed by the Great Depression. By 1930, one out of four Americans was out of work.

During this severe economic downturn, Hill received a letter from the White House requesting his help. This was in 1933, right after Franklin D. Roosevelt had taken office. Hill provided President Roosevelt with suggestions for the president's famous speeches, which were given in an attempt to lift the spirits of a downcast nation. For his dedication to the president's cause, Hill won much admiration.

Following his work with the Roosevelt Administration, Hill increasingly found himself in demand for speeches and lectures. And with the popularity of *The Law of Success*, Hill was busier than ever, traveling all over the country on lecture tours.

Think and Grow Rich

In 1937, Hill was ready to publish his most famous book, *Think and Grow Rich*, which he originally considered titling "The Thirteen Steps to Riches." After the third rewrite, Hill began searching for a publisher. And who better to present the newly rewritten work to than Andrew Pelton, who had published *The Law of Success*, making both himself and Hill small fortunes?

Pelton agreed to publish the book and initially wanted to title it "Use Your Noodle to Win More Boodle." However, with Hill's persuasion the book was published as *Think and Grow Rich*, and it was an instant success.

The publisher priced the book at $2.50 a copy, which was a considerable amount in 1937. Even with a serious economic depression the book managed to sell all five thousand copies in the first print run in a manner of weeks. Shortly after *Think and Grow Rich* was published, an insurance company purchased five thousand copies leading to additional printings of over thirty thousand copies by August of 1937.

Over a million copies of the book sold before the Great Depression was over. Within fifty years over twenty million copies had been sold. Over sixty million copies have been sold throughout the world. *Think and Grow Rich* has proven to be the best-selling self-help book ever written.

There are many reasons why *Think and Grow Rich* became an immediate bestseller, such as the need of people to be inspired and their desire to be successful. But surely the best reason the book continues to attract readers is that the information was derived from the original material of *The Law of Success*. It was inspired by Andrew Carnegie and based on twenty years of interviews and research into what makes it possible for people to become successful. The research Hill conducted for *The Law of Success* and *Think and Grow Rich* produced books that are among the most original works in the personal-development genre.

In 1938, a copy of *Think and Grow Rich* was given to an insurance salesman from Chicago by the name of W. Clement Stone, who immediately became interested in the philosophy outlined in the book. Stone was so successful in the use of *Think and Grow Rich* that within one year his sales grew ten times from the previous year.

By 1941 Hill had added to his popularity by joining forces with Dr. William Plumer Jacobs, president of Presbyterian College, owner of Jacobs Press, and public relations adviser to a group of South Carolina textile firms. Hill had met Jacobs while he was lecturing in Atlanta, Georgia, in 1940. Their business venture required that Hill move to Clinton, South Carolina, where Jacobs resided.

The project called for Hill to rewrite his personal achievement philosophy as a self-help course and create a lecture series to be called "The Philosophy of Achievement."

It would first be presented at the Presbyterian College. Next, the lectures would be delivered in schools, towns, and factories throughout South Carolina and other states in the South. The idea was to attract industries from the North to relocate to the South.

It took Hill months to rewrite his philosophy of success, and he ended up with seventeen small books, averaging about one hundred pages each, called *Mental Dynamite*. Hill's lectures became very popular, and *Mental Dynamite* was published by Jacobs Press.

In 1943, Hill took his lecture series on the road to California, and it quickly attracted many followers. During this period Hill received an honorary doctor of literature degree from Pacific International University.

The Philosophy of Success

In 1947, he launched a talk show with KFWB Radio in Hollywood, California. For three years, hundreds of thousands of people had the opportunity to hear Hill and his philosophy of success. It was said of him that in his early sixties, he looked forty-five and had the charm of a thirty-five-year-old and a teenager's energy. Hill's radio show led to more speaking jobs at companies and business groups.

At the age of sixty-seven, a still active Hill fulfilled a promise to deliver a speech in Chicago at the request of a local dentist. This speech at the dental convention would change Hill's life and the lives of millions of others.

In the audience was a businessman by the name of W. Clement Stone who had introduced the dentist to *Think and Grow Rich* years earlier. Hill had been enjoying a partial retirement, but Stone challenged Hill to spread the message of success with his help.

Stone and Hill formed the Napoleon Hill Associates to approach sales groups with the message of success. Stone would later remark that he "really hit the jackpot with Napoleon Hill." Together, Stone and Hill produced books, courses, lectures, radio shows, and eventually television programs.

Within two years after starting together, they published the *Science of Success* textbook, which was later renamed the *PMA: Science of Success* course.

Throughout the rest of their lives, Napoleon Hill and W. Clement Stone continued their mission of spreading success philosophy to help others:

In 1953, Stone and Hill published *How to Raise Your Own Salary.*

In 1954, Stone and Hill began publication of a small magazine, *Success Unlimited.* Each issue carried messages of inspiration from the two businessmen.

In 1959, when Hill had already celebrated his seventy-fifth birthday, he was still giving speeches, traveling to places like Puerto Rico, Australia, and New Zealand. These lectures were usually conducted jointly with Stone.

In 1960, Hill and Stone coauthored a new book, *Success Through a Positive Mental Attitude,* which was an instant classic in the self-help field and quickly sold over six hundred thousand copies in the United States. *Success Through a Positive Mental Attitude* has been published throughout the world and still sells well today.

In 1962, Hill and his last wife, Annie Lou, formed the Napoleon Hill Foundation. A product of the thinking of the wealthiest men in America, the foundation is unique because it is dedicated to promoting personal achievement and to inspiring individuals to overcome obstacles in order to succeed.

In 1967, at the age of eighty-four, Hill published *Grow Rich with Peace of Mind*.

Along with Stone, the original trustees of the Napoleon Hill Foundation included Dr. Charles Johnson, MD; the nephew of Annie Lou Hill; and West Virginia senator Jennings Randolph, whose support of Hill began when Hill gave the address at Randolph's graduation at Salem College in 1922.

Michael J. Ritt Jr., who worked for fifty-two years as a vice president at Stone's company, Combined Insurance, traveled with Stone and Hill writing, promoting, and recording the two great men's work. Ritt Jr. became the first executive director of the Napoleon Hill Foundation.

Today the Napoleon Hill Foundation continues the work Hill began over one hundred years ago. Hill and Stone would be pleased to realize the current popularity of their work all over the world.

It is our sincere hope that you will also benefit from these words spoken many years ago, but timeless in their wisdom. Please note that I have written comments preceding the speeches and letters as introductions and to provide contextual background information.

We are pleased to present in the pages that follow, this never-before-published collection of the greatest speeches of the one and only, Napoleon Hill.

—DON M. GREEN, Director
Napoleon Hill Foundation

In 1917, Napoleon Hill was operating the George Washington Institute in Chicago. Among the topics Hill lectured on at the school were "Lessons on Selling," "Applied Psychology," "What I Learned from Analyzing Ten Thousand People," and "The Man Who Has Had No Chance." Hill was truly knowledgeable about each of the subjects on which he lectured. "Lessons on Selling" was no doubt influenced by his experience coaching salespeople. Followers of Hill's career know that he made a living throughout most of his life teaching sales techniques. Many leading salespeople such as Jeffrey Gitomer, known for his many best-selling books on sales like *Little Red Book of Selling*, consider Hill's writings on sales to be his best work.

Hill's lessons on applied psychology owe their genesis to his vast study of and fascination with the subject, especially the work of Dr. Warren Hilton, AB, LLB, founder of the Society of Applied Psychology. Dr. Hilton wrote a twelve-volume set of books in 1914 from which Hill often quoted.

This speech, "What I Learned from Analyzing Ten Thousand People," is the direct result of work that began with Andrew Carnegie in 1908. While

Hill interviewed Carnegie, Thomas Edison, George Eastman, Henry Ford, and many of the other most prosperous men of his day to discover their methods for success, Hill also conducted countless interviews to learn why people fail. Often these took the form of questionnaires that were either passed out at lectures and classes or circulated through the mail.

Hill prepared his lectures on an old L. C. Smith typewriter and then gave copies to his students at the George Washington Institute. This lesson was given in 1917. Signed "Napoleon," it has existed in the archives of the Napoleon Hill Foundation for over ninety years.

In his lecture "What I Learned from Analyzing Ten Thousand People," Hill summarizes the five chief requisites for success. Hill lists "self-confidence" and "enthusiasm" as the most important traits for success. The third requisite needed for success was a "definite working plan," or what he alternately refers to as a "chief aim in life." Today, we might use the term "worthwhile goal." The fourth requisite was "the habit of performing more service than you are actually paid for." This requisite informed his principle Going the Extra Mile, which involves someone doing something without permission, going above and beyond without explicit instructions for doing so. Hill listed "concentration" as the fifth requisite, advising that it is necessary for success in any undertaking.

DON GREEN

What I Learned from Analyzing Ten Thousand People

by
Napoleon Hill

During the past eight years I have analyzed over ten thousand men and women who were earnestly seeking their proper niche in the world's work. Incidentally, through my work I have discovered some of the fundamental qualities without which no human being can hope for success. Five of these are mentioned in this article.

I have also discovered some of the things that break men's hearts and send them to the scrap heap of human failures. It is my sincere hope that every person who reads this article may profit by one or more of the points that it covers. I am placing the results of my discoveries in print solely out of my deep desire to make life's pathway just a little smoother for my fellow man.

It is my purpose to pass on to you, in as few words as possible, that portion of my discoveries which I believe will aid you in *planning* and *achieving* your "chief aim" in life, whatever that may be. I shall not preach to you. Whatever suggestions I make are based upon discoveries that I have made in my work.

I believe it befitting to state that twenty years ago I was working as a laborer, at wages of a dollar a day. I had no home and no friends. I had but little education. My future then looked very unpromising. I was downcast in spirit. I had no ambition. I had no definite purpose in life. All around me I saw men, some young and some old, who were whipped—just as I felt that I was. I absorbed my environment as a sponge absorbs water. I became a part of the daily routine in which I lived.

It had never occurred to me that I could ever amount to anything. I believed my lot in life was to be that of a laborer. I was just like a horse that has had the bit slipped into its mouth and the saddle buckled on its back.

Here is the turning point in my career. Note it well! A chance remark, no doubt made in a half-jocular way, caused me to throw the bit out of my mouth, kick off the saddle, and "run away" as young horses sometimes do. That remark was made by a farmer with whom I lived. I shall never forget it if I live to be a hundred because it has partly bridged the gap over that awful chasm which nearly all human beings want to cross: *failure!*

The remark was this: "You are a bright boy. What a pity you are not in school instead of at work as a laborer at a dollar a day!"

"You are a bright boy!" These were the sweetest words I have ever heard.

That remark aroused in me the *first ambition* I had ever felt, and, incidentally, it is directly responsible for the Personal Analysis system that I have worked out. No one had ever hinted to me before that I was "bright." I had always imagined I was exceedingly dull. In fact, I had been told that I was a dunce. As a boy I was defeated in everything I undertook, largely because those with whom I associated ridiculed me and discouraged me from engaging in the things that interested me most. My work was selected for me, my studies were selected for me, and my play, well, I was taught that play was a waste of time.

With this firsthand knowledge of the great handicap under which the average person starts out in life as a working basis, I began, many years ago, to work out a system for helping people "find themselves" as early in life as possible. My efforts have yielded splendid returns, for I have helped many find the work for which they were most suited, and I have started them on the road to happiness and success. I have helped more than a few to acquire the qualities for success that are mentioned in this article.

The First Two Success Requisites

With this prelude I shall tell you first what I believe to be the two most important of the five chief requisites for success. These are *self-confidence* and *enthusiasm*. The other three I will mention later.

Fully ninety percent of those ten thousand people whom I have analyzed were lacking in these two qualities. I have analyzed men who were strong in both body and mind—men who were well educated, some of them college graduates, who were as helpless as I was the day the farmer made the remark, "You are a bright boy."

My first task in advising people who lack self-confidence is to save them from themselves. Figuratively speaking, they must be taken out into the field and allowed to "run away," just as a horse might do. They must discover their real strength. They must learn that their weakness exists nowhere except in their own deceptive imaginations. The manner in which I set people right in this respect must vary with each individual.

The difference between the man who achieves success and the man who does not is not necessarily in brain capacity. More often the difference is in the use men make of their latent ability. I do not merely suspect that this is true—I know it is! I have gained this knowledge from actual experience in analyzing men. Usually the man who develops and uses all of his latent powers is a man who has plenty of self-confidence.

What is self-confidence? I will tell you what it is: it is the little glass window through which you may look and see the real manpower within your body. Self-confidence is self-discovery—finding out who you are and what you can do. It is the banishment of fear. It is the acquirement of mental courage. It is the turning on of the light of human intelligence through the use of common sense.

It was self-confidence, plus enthusiasm and concentration that caused the birth of the world's greatest inventions: the incandescent electric light, the automobile, the talking machine, the aeroplane, the moving picture, and all the other great mechanical creations.

> *Self-confidence is an essential quality for all worthwhile accomplishments.*

Self-confidence, then, is an essential quality for all worthwhile accomplishments. Yet, it is the quality in which most of us are weakest—not a weakness that many of us acknowledge, but it exists just the same. A man without self-confidence is like a ship without a rudder: he wastes his time without moving in the right direction.

I wish I might be able to tell you exactly how to acquire full self-confidence. That would be a big undertaking. I will give you this suggestion, however: I made my first steps in the direction of self-confidence the day I first heard the words, "You are a bright boy." That was the first time I had ever felt ambition tugging at my coat sleeve, and with it, apparently, came self-confidence.

One of my very close friends became a successful dentist after he had reached the age of thirty-five as a result of a remark made by his wife. He was examining his wife's false teeth when his wife said to him, "You could make a set of teeth like that." He began that very day to try, and soon he stepped from unsuccessful farming to successful dentistry.

In my resident class is a young man who has had splendid educational advantages, but until recently he was the poorest student in the class. He had plenty of ability, but he lacked the self-confidence with which to put it to work. A few weeks ago, he met a young lady with whom he fell in love. She told him she *believed in him*. He believed her, and as a result, he commenced to gain self-confidence. The short period of three weeks has completely transformed him. He is now one of our best students.

It is remarkable what clothes have to do with building self-confidence. A man came to me for analysis not long ago. He had been earning a good salary, but conditions for which he was in no way responsible caused him to be let go. I asked him how much money he had, and he said, "Seventy-five dollars." I told him to invest one-third of it in a new suit of clothes. He demurred on the ground that he "couldn't afford it." But I insisted and went with him to buy the clothes. Then I insisted on his going to the cobbler's and having the heels of his shoes straightened up. Then I persuaded him to have his shoes shined and to get a clean shave and a haircut. I then sent him to see the president of a large corporation, who employed him at three thousand dollars a year.

If I had sent him to the interview with the president of that corporation without the new suit and the cleanup, he wouldn't have gotten the position, in all probability, because he would not have had the proper self-confidence. Good clothes, clean linen, polished shoes, and a clean shave are not luxuries—they are a necessity to the man who comes in contact with the business public.

These are just a few of the ways in which I know that people have made the first step toward acquiring self-confidence. I have noticed that there is no self-confidence without ambition. They go hand in hand.

The Second Success Requisite

The second requisite for success is *enthusiasm*, that great dynamic force which puts self-confidence into action. Enthusiasm may be likened to the steam that runs the locomotive. The most powerful locomotive ever built might stand upon the side-track with coal in the bunker and the engineer in the cab, but if there is no steam, the wheels will not turn—there is no action.

It is exactly the same with the human machine. If there is no enthusiasm, there is little or no action. Lack of these qualities—self-confidence and enthusiasm—stands between the great majority of men and success. This statement is no mere conjecture upon my part. I have proven it in thousands of cases. I am proving it in more than a hundred cases a week today. Enthusiasm is something that cannot be counterfeited. Only the real article will fill the bill. Enthusiasm usually comes automatically when you find the vocation into which you can pitch your whole heart and soul—the work you love best.

The Third Success Requisite

The third requisite for success is *a definite working plan*—the habit of working with a "chief aim" in life.

From my work as a vocational director I have learned that most people have no such plan. Men who are working without a well-defined plan—without a predetermined objective—are going nowhere in particular, and most of them are getting nowhere. In my Personal Analysis Chart, which all whom I examine must fill out, is this question: *"What is your chief aim in life?"*

An actual tabulation of answers to this question shows that only one out of every fifty has any "chief aim." But few have any sort of a real aim, "chief" or otherwise. Yet, nearly all whom I have analyzed expect to succeed. Just when, or how, or in what work, the majority of them do not undertake to say.

A few weeks ago I stood and watched some men at work on a skyscraper. It was a massive building, towering far above the tops of the other buildings nearby. An elevator descended, took on a small steel beam, hoisted it into position, and the workmen soon made it a permanent part of that great building.

Then this thought came to me: this building is only the sum total of brick, lumber, steel beams, and building materials, put together according to a definite *plan*! The same thought may be applied when we analyze men who are succeeding. The man who is holding a "big position" made that position for himself out of a number of smaller tasks well performed.

Nearly every man wants a "big position," yet not one out of a hundred, even though he may be competent, knows how to get it. A "big position" is not something that we find hanging on a bush ready to be plucked off through "pull" by the first person who comes along. It is the sum total of a number of smaller positions or tasks that we have efficiently filled—not necessarily with different firms, but, as often as otherwise, in the employment of one firm. A big position is built just as we build a big skyscraper—by first formulating a definite plan and then building according to that plan, step by step.

The possible exception to this rule is the man who gets into a "big position" through "pull." There are exceptions to most rules, but the question to ask yourself is this: "Am I willing to go through life and take a chance on getting ahead on 'pull'?" Look about you, and I daresay you will find that for every man who is succeeding by "pull," you may find a hundred who are succeeding by "push"!

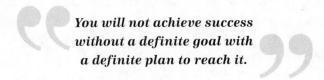

You will not achieve success without a definite goal with a definite plan to reach it.

There are varying degrees of success, just as there are different ideas as to what success is, but whether your idea of success is the accumulation of wealth or the rendering of some great service to mankind or both, you will not likely achieve it unless you have a "chief aim"—a definite goal with a definite plan mapped out for reaching it.

No architect ever started a building until he had first created a perfect picture of it in his mind and then carefully transferred the detail of the picture to a blueprint. And no human being may hope to build a worthwhile success until he has planned the building and decided what it shall be.

I have found through my work as a vocational director that only one out of a hundred has planned ahead and decided just what he will be doing a year in advance. Only one out of a thousand has planned ahead for five years, and I have yet to find the first person who has planned ahead for ten years!

Do you wonder, then, why ninety-five percent of the people of the world are working for the other five percent? Do you wonder why so many men and women go through life without accumulating anything for old age? Have you ever stopped to wonder why it is that a few men get ahead while the great mass are failures?

It will pay you to throw the spotlight on yourself and see how you measure up as to self-confidence, enthusiasm, and definite purpose or "chief aim" in life.

Selecting a Vocation

A very large proportion of the people whom I have analyzed are in positions that they hold, not by selection, but by chance. Even those who are following vocations that they deliberately chose, in the majority of cases, have not observed even the most elementary rules of self-analysis. They have never stopped to find out whether or not the work in which they are engaged is the work for which they are best fitted by nature and education.

For example, a young man whom I recently analyzed had prepared himself for the practice of law but had made an utter failure of that profession. He failed, first, because he did not like the profession after he got into it; secondly, because he had absolutely no native ability for that profession. He was badly deformed physically and, as a consequence, made a very poor impression before courts and juries. He lacked enthusiasm and that dynamic force which we call "personality," without which he could not hope to succeed as a lawyer. Such a person might succeed to some extent as an advisory counsel or "office lawyer" but not as a trial lawyer, where a strong personality and the ability to speak with force and conviction count for so much.

The surprising part of this particular case was the fact that this man had never understood just why he did not succeed in the practice of law. It seemed simple enough to him after I had pointed out the negative qualities that I believed had stood between him and success. When I asked him how he came to take up law, he replied, "Well, I just had a hunch that I would like it!"

"I just had a hunch that I would like it!" Selecting your life's work on a "hunch" is a dangerous thing. You wouldn't purchase a racehorse on a "hunch"; you would want to see him perform on the track. You wouldn't purchase a bird dog on a "hunch"; you would want to see him in action or know something of his pedigree. If you selected a bird dog in this haphazard way, you might find yourself trying to set birds with a bull pup!

A court reporter whom I analyzed said to me: "My fifteen years of experience have proven to me that a jury seldom tries the defendant, but instead, they try the lawyers in the case. The lawyer who makes the best impression generally wins." Everyone who is familiar with court actions knows that this is too often true. You can see, therefore, what an important part "personality" plays in the practice of law.

My experience as a vocational director has convinced me that a very large number of business failures are due to the fact that men select partners and enter business projects on "hunches." Men who would become competent engineers enter the grocery business, and vice versa—men who probably would succeed in the grocery business go into engineering. The result in both cases usually is failure.

Then another common mistake that men make is in selecting partners among their friends and those who are their exact counterparts in training, temperament, etc. A few years ago three young men organized a corporation and went into business. They had all been successful executives in the employ of a corporation engaged in the same business that they entered for themselves. They had the necessary capital, but they made one fatal mistake: they failed to take into the firm a competent sales manager. These young men were excellent financiers, all of them, but they needed something more than financiers. They needed "business"! An ideal organization could have been made up by selecting one financial man, one competent sales manager, and one experienced buyer. Then, in selecting their help, they would have profited by employing men who would have brought to the firm some ability that the members themselves did not possess.

Every firm ought to have men of opposite types, temperaments, and abilities. One type should correspond to the balance wheel, while the other should represent the generator. The composite of these two types would make an ideal organization.

Mr. Carnegie says that his success is due largely to his ability to pick men. Mr. Frank A. Vanderlip and Mr. John D. Rockefeller say the same. If you will stop and analyze all successful men you know, you will probably find that they either possess all the requisites for success in the business in which they are engaged or they know how to select men who will supply what they lack—men who are their opposites in nearly every particular.

Probably fifty percent of those who call themselves salesmen are of poor personal appearance, have weak faces, and speak without force. A salesman conveys to his prospective buyer a positive or negative influence according to his own personality and manner of approach in presenting his case. A man who is badly deformed, or the man who suffers from impediment of speech or otherwise makes a negative appearance, had better not take up oral salesmanship. If he can hide behind the written page, he may succeed—but in person, never!

It is usually the minister's personal appearance and the manner in which he delivers his message that wins his followers. If you should read one of Billy Sunday's sermons before having heard him, you would wonder how he was able to sway thousands as he does. Without his pleasing personality and his remarkable and characteristic manner of delivery, his sermons would seem cold and undignified, if not actually repulsive.

The Fourth Success Requisite

The fourth success requisite is *the habit of performing more service than you are actually paid for.* It is the practice of the majority of men to perform no more service than they feel they are being paid to perform. Fully eighty percent of all whom I have analyzed were suffering on account of this great mistake.

You need have no fear of competition from the man who says, "I'm not paid to do that, therefore I'll not do it." He will never be a dangerous competitor for your job. But watch out for the fellow who does not let his pick hang in the air when the whistle blows or the man who stays at his desk or work bench until his work is finished—watch out that such a fellow does not "challenge you at the post and pass you at the grandstand," as Andrew Carnegie said.

Before mentioning the fifth and last requisite for success, I shall ask your indulgence while I digress for just a few moments. After I had commenced work on this article, I decided to have the five points which I am covering put to the acid test to see whether or not they would square up with the experience of other vocational directors. I took the manuscript to Dr. J. M. Fitzgerald of Chicago, who is probably the most able vocational director in the world.

Dr. Fitzgerald went over the manuscript with me word for word, and I have his permission to quote him as saying that he fully endorses the five chief points covered by this article. He says that they square up with his own experience exactly. But before we went over the manuscript, I asked Dr. Fitzgerald to state the chief negative qualities that he had discovered to be standing as barriers between those whom he had analyzed and success. His reply was quick and concise, as follows:

1. Lack of self-discernment: the lack of ability upon the part of most men to analyze themselves and find the work for which they are best prepared.

2. Lack of intensified concentration and the disposition not to put more into their work than they expect to get out of it.

3. Lack of moral self-control.

Dr. Fitzgerald has analyzed in person more than fifteen thousand men and women. Many of the largest corporations of the Midwest will not employ a man for any important position until he has been analyzed by Dr. Fitzgerald. He has taken men from the bookkeeper's desk and enabled them to become successful executives. He has converted clerks into managers in much less time than is ordinarily required, merely by having started them in the right direction through accurate personal analysis.

I mention these details concerning Dr. Fitzgerald's work because I want you to feel that my own experience, as stated in this article, is not mere conjecture on my part—that it is authentic and that it has the endorsement of the world's greatest personal analyst. Bear in mind that the five chief points covered by this article have been discovered, classified, and charted from the personal analysis of twenty-five thousand people, ten thousand of whom I have analyzed and fifteen thousand of whom were analyzed by Dr. Fitzgerald!

The Fifth Success Requisite

This brings me to the fifth and last success requisite which I have discovered through my work as a vocational director. I have mentioned it before and I shall mention it many times in the future because it is one of the most important of the five points covered in this article.

The last success requisite is *concentration!*

You might as well make up your mind right here and now that you must concentrate if you want to succeed in any undertaking.

You may have all the knowledge you need for success in any undertaking—you may be a walking encyclopedia of information, you may be well educated, you may be experienced—but if you do not direct these energies systematically, they will be of little real use to either you or the world.

We have a man here in the school who is a genius in many respects. He is a splendid carpenter. He is also one of best electricians I ever saw. He is a splendid plumber. As an engineer, few can equal him. He is an artist with a paintbrush. He is a splendid decorator, and so on, ad infinitum, but the fact still remains that he is working for eighteen dollars a week!

If he devoted all of his time to electrical work, he could easily command thirty dollars a week or more. But, he insists on having a hand in everything that comes along. His power to concentrate is nil!

Learn to Concentrate

I need cite no further evidence that the power of concentration is essential to success. You know that it is as well as I do. What you probably are most interested in is, *"How may I learn to concentrate?"*

I gave you a part of my own version of how to learn to concentrate in the story entitled "The Great Magic Key to Success." Now I shall give you the more scientific explanation of concentration by one of the best-known psychologists in America, Dr. Warren Hilton, in the following words *(Before you read what Dr. Hilton has to say, I want you to know that his explanations have the endorsement of such well-known men as the late Professor Hugo Münsterberg of Harvard University, Professor George Trumbull Ladd of Yale University, Professor Knight Dunlap of Johns Hopkins University, and many other noted psychologists and scientists. His explanations are based upon physiological as well as psychological tests made in the laboratory of the Society of Applied Psychology):*

Concentration, speaking generally, is defined as "the act of bringing together at one center or focus." Mental concentration is therefore a focusing of the mind upon one object or point.

There is nothing abnormal about the sort of concentration to which we refer. Your individual character or personality is made up simply of the progressive results of your trained habits of concentration of attention. Every conviction that you have on any subject, from religion to politics, is the outgrowth of the ways in which you have concentrated your attention.

Every conviction thus acquired is wrapped up and stowed away in some thought complex of the past. It is a part of your personality. It will resist, with all the might of its innate energy, the establishment in your mind of any contrary beliefs.

The admonitions of a mother may be so implanted in the mind of her boy that all the contrary leanings and impulses will be inhibited. No amount of argument will dispel the faith that religion has fixed in the mind of the true convert. Only the strongest evidence will overcome a man's confidence in the character of an accused friend.

Life is made up of experiences. *And the influence of every experience upon your conduct and character depends upon the degree of concentration of attention with which it is received.*

And so every idea in memory has a tendency to direct the mind toward those things that are associated with it in time or place or otherwise, and the extent of its influence depends upon its vividness. Every soft inflection in the well-remembered voice of one you love has a tendency to concentrate the activities of your consciousness upon those things that are associated with the object of your affections. Every advertisement, every shop-window display, every prospectus, every business man's artifice, every salesman's lure, depends for its effectiveness upon the extent of its concentrating influence, the extent to which it is able to bring about a concentration of attention in those to whom it is addressed.

The mere presence of an idea in consciousness is not concentration. If you suggest to one that a white mist floating across a meadow is a wraith, the idea will be momentarily active in his consciousness, and yet you may have simply succeeded in directing his ordinary attention to an abstract conception. But if he is a believer in spirits and comes away shaken with terror and convinced that he has actually seen a ghost, then there has been a concentration of his consciousness in a scientific sense.

Not every idea presented to consciousness constitutes belief or results in action. In the first instance, the thought of the "ghost" was active in the man's mind, *but other conflicting ideas and impulses were simultaneously present denying its reality.* In the second instance, however, his consciousness was given over wholly to the idea of a "ghost" that you presented to him. *There were present no inhibitory ideas and impulses.* He accepted the thought and believed in the reality of it, and, giving free rein to his impulses, he acted accordingly.

Concentration technically interpreted necessarily implies, then, belief in the idea that is the subject of concentration. And this belief releases the impulses for appropriate muscular responses.

How, then, shall we define concentration? Simply thus: *Concentration is such a focusing of consciousness upon an idea that if complete it will overcome all conflicting ideas and will result in a belief that will control conduct.*

When we say "complete," we mean that the idea in question must hold *undisputed sway* in consciousness. When this occurs, the idea will be so assimilated as to become incorporated as a part of the personality. You accept it as truth. You believe in it. This belief becomes an element of your personality. It is "your own."

And so it comes about that efficient concentration necessarily results in *belief* coupled with such *muscular activity* as accords with or tends to bring about the realization of that belief. *An overmastering conviction and an efficient will are therefore the immediate results of complete concentration.*

Concentration will be of value to you in two ways:

1.   *It will give you a minute and specialized knowledge of things and make you an expert in your line.*

It is related of Agassiz that he used to lock a student up in a room day after day with a turtle's head and not release him until he had learned everything there was to know about it. Some achieved this happy result after months of lonely contemplation. Others never did succeed. The successful ones had formed the habit of concentration. They deserved the title of "naturalist" for which Agassiz was fitting them. The unsuccessful ones were forever "blotted from the book of honor and life."

Learn, then, to concentrate, for without it you can pretend to no real knowledge of anything. This is an age of specialists, and the essence of specialization is the acquiring of a minute knowledge of one thing.

Few people realize the immense part that the quality of thoroughness plays in the life of the successful man. The man of millions has generally earned every dollar of his money by doing everything he undertook just a little better than the next man.

The average man is superficial. His motto is "To seem, not to be." He is willing to "let well enough alone," and has a very modest conception of what "well enough" is. His competitor needs only a little of the leaven of thoroughness to outstrip him.

What you do today is but practice for what you are going to do tomorrow, and if you do whatever you undertake as if your life depended on the issue, your capabilities for greater things will grow in proportion.

The fact is that thoroughness is the distinguishing trait of the super-man. And the secret of thoroughness is mental concentration.

2.   (And this point is much the more important of the two.) *Concentration, whether you will or not,*

will necessarily result in your driving ahead with all your energy in pursuit of a given end until your point is gained.

The stream of your consciousness is a living current. It is a seething, swirling torrent of activity.

Look within and see what is taking place at this moment. You find yourself making resemblances, noting distinctions, associating one thing with another, and selecting and attending to certain ideas, feelings, and impulses while ignoring a multitude of others.

This is the thing called consciousness. It is not an aimless current. It does not flow through the hills and valleys of life adapting itself to the contours of the physical environment. It is a stream that can, if need be, flow uphill. It is consciousness with a "will." It is consciousness that labors to preserve you, to promote your free development, and to further your practical success.

Make a Practice

Make a practice of concentrating upon matters pertaining to a single interest, and you will become *absorbed in it as an ideal*. You will acquire a standard by which to appraise the value to you of the facts of your life.

Make a practice of concentrating upon a single interest, and you will acquire a constant and completely "possessing" and automatic *inhibitory* power.

You will without thinking refrain from many useless activities. You will refrain from indulgence in pleasures and recreations that would interfere with the accomplishment of your main purpose. You will refrain from wasteful expenditure of your emotions. You will save from a single hour of anger enough energy for a successful day.

Make a practice of concentrating upon a single interest, and you will acquire an ideal that will automatically operate the levers of inner control.

You will acquire a mental machine operating economically, a well-oiled machine that will work automatically, without friction, without effort, almost without thought.

This does not mean that you will be left without the passions that kindle the fires of heroic achievement. Concentration in its highest sense means *absorbing, passionate devotion to a cause.* It means the state of mind of men whom St. Paul would describe as "fervent"—literally "boiling in spirit."

Absolute concentration means the massing of every atom of individual human energy upon a single purpose. It is the acme of efficiency.

Commonly your emotions and desires scatter your energies and exhaust you to no purpose.

Organize and concentrate these powers, and the only question remaining unanswered is "What goal shall I win?"

Be a man of concentration, and you will be a man of purpose, with faith in the attainment of that purpose.

Be a man of concentration, and you will possess a mental co-ordination, harmony, and unity that will lift you above petty annoyances and free you from such impediments as moods and restlessness and discontent.

Concentrate upon a single purpose. Keep your ideals before you. You cannot then fail to focus all your activities upon the desired end. *Only those muscular impulses will find release in actions that are associated with the thought of your desire.*

Concentrate upon a single purpose, and you will be possessed of an ideal by which to judge the opportunities of your life. You will shrewdly, naturally, and unhesitatingly select those that will contribute to your purpose. You will wisely choose certain pleasures and recreations and discard others. You will have an unerring gauge by which to distinguish luxuries from necessities.

Concentrate upon a single purpose, and, often when you least expect it, but surely, surely, the time will come when you will see and grasp your chance and strike in with a winning stroke.

This is the law of success. This is what Lincoln really meant, although it may not have occurred to him in just that form, when he said, "I will study and prepare myself and then some day my chance will come."

Would you sway the minds of others? The same principle applies. The man you are to meet is a problem to be solved. Employ the method of Agassiz. Your man has tastes, tendencies, moods, habits, and interests that you must consider. He has animosities, determinations, prejudices, inertias, and resistances that must be taken into account. Like yourself, he is a living consciousness, a creature of impulses and inhibitions.

Do not try to batter through his inhibitions. Do not employ coercive methods.

Your task is to soothe him into indifference as to all things that tend to inhibit action along desired lines. Do not waste your time in trying to put out of his mind ideas hostile to your purpose.

His consciousness is a thing of incessant activity. It must be kept busy. The way to bar out undesirable thought is to fill his mind with other things. Therefore, *concentrate his attention upon you and your demands.* This done, your cause is gained. You have won the day.

"Your ability to move things," says Waldo P. Warren, "depends largely on where you take hold. I shall never forget the first time I saw the great Ferris wheel—that wonder of two world's fairs.

"What impressed me most was not its magnitude, but the fact that, in spite of its gigantic size, it required only a comparatively small engine to run it. For unlike most wheels the power was not applied at the center, but at the circumference, thus utilizing the extraordinary leverage of one hundred and eighty feet. The same force, if exerted at the axle, would have been powerless to move the wheel a single inch.

"The lever principle is not confined to mechanical things—it is one of the great fundamental ideas which humanity has discovered.

"When the progress of your campaign is beset with obstacles, whether ignorance, prejudice, injustice, or delay, remember the lever principle. Somewhere there is a move that you can make that will set in motion a chain of events that will eventually move even the greatest obstacle. Don't strain at the hub of the ponderous wheel—move a cog that fits into the rim."

In influencing others, just as in mastering yourself, the true test of efficiency, the secret of success, lies in the ability to concentrate the attention.[1]

The Art of Concentration

"Ah, but how to concentrate!" you may say. "So far from being able to concentrate the attention of others, I have never been able to do any concentrating of my own."

Be patient, friend! You shall learn the art of concentration. There are *methods* and *devices* that, if faithfully employed, put this power within reach of everyone. But first you must realize the wide reach of this mighty weapon. You must know something of the processes and principles underlying its scientific use.

We want you to approach these great truths in a spirit of reverence and awe; this not alone because of their intrinsic worth, but also because of their influence in molding the history of men. For the world owes all that is great in religion, in war, in art, in science, in all noble endeavor, to concentration, *the concentration of divine talents with unswerving faith upon a lofty purpose.*

It was concentration that made Alexander master of the world, sighing for more worlds to conquer. It was concentration that made Confucius devote his life through incalculable suffering to great teachings, and made Socrates prefer the cup of hemlock to the repudiation of his principles. It created Zoroaster, farther back then memory. It created Mohammed, the prophet of Arabia. And with its unwavering light came the founder of Christianity, the Nazarene.

Here in America, it was concentration that gave us Washington, that inspired Lincoln. It was concentration that built the first steamboat, that invented the cotton gin, that discovered the secret of telegraphy, that made Edison the "wizard of electricity." It was concentration that lifted Rockefeller and Morgan to the pinnacles of opulent power. It was concentration, nationwide and based upon an enduring faith, that preserved our national integrity through the scouring fire of internecine strife.

> *Concentration lifted Rockefeller and Morgan to the pinnacles of opulent power.*

In none of these instances was there any *deliberate* concentration of mental forces. The vast and overpowering *desire* was in each case brought about by other influences than the action of the individual will.

Yet the study and practice of deliberate concentration, of voluntary concentration, of *concentration as an art* is no new thing. In various guises it has appeared upon the stage of history among all races and nations and in all times since the world was young.

The practice of concentration as an art has heretofore always been shrouded in occultism and mystery. This is because its devotees have had merely an empirical knowledge of the subject. They have observed what could be accomplished by concentrative devices and methods, but they have had no comprehension of the *reason* for the results they observed. Standing back in astonishment at the wonders they were able to work, and unable to explain these occurrences in any rational way, they ascribed the results to miraculous or supernatural agencies.

In all ages and in all climes, man has bowed before an Intelligent Power capable of producing or healing diseases in the human body and capable of bestowing or withholding peace and plenty. The character of this unseen and intangible Force has varied with different races of men and different periods of their history. But always and everywhere we find the startling fact that all the peoples of the earth, civilized and uncivilized, have used, and still do use, generically, the same methods of appealing to this invisible Power.

The Chaldean seer gazed into the eye of a glittering gem until a trance ensued in which he could divine the purposes of the Mighty. So did the Egyptian priest, the Persian magi, and the Hindu fakir, all of whom still bring themselves to a trancelike state of fixation of gaze. That strange sect of early Christians known as Taskodrugites accomplished the same results during prayer by looking fixedly at the forefinger held close before the face and pointing at the nose. The monks of the Greek Church in the convent of Mount Athos sought freedom from the distractions of a noisy world and entered into communion with the Holy Spirit by gazing steadily at their umbilicus. The fetish worshiper fixes his fascinated eye upon a stick or stone in which dwells for him all power and beneficence. The Annamite gazes with wondering trust at two burning sticks fastened behind the left ear of the magician who slowly and impressively revolves upon his heel.

Charms and idolatrous ceremonies, occult "mysteries" and religious practices, witches' incantations and priestly sacrifices, hideous noises and diabolical makeup of the "medicine man" and "voodoo doctor," all are but ways and means devised by men to thwart the efforts of evil spirits and conciliate the good.

And *all* have two elements in common. First, they serve to *grip the interest of the faithful one.* Second, having focused his attention, they then *direct it toward belief in the realization of a hope*; they play it like a calcium light upon the consummation so devoutly wished.

All are but different devices for bringing about that mental concentration which we have defined as the overmastering focusing of consciousness upon the *belief* in an idea.

> *Concentration is the over-mastering focusing of consciousness upon the belief in an idea.*

The prayer of pious persons, the "yoga" of the Hindu, the "silence" of the disciple of "New Thought," the meditation of the philosopher, *all* find their elements of efficacious truth in this basic principle. From the routine telling of beads of orthodox Christians to the "disembodied" soul of the Hindu "adept," *all* are but manifestations and degrees of mental concentration.

Consider the occultism of the Hindu now in such vogue. "Yoga," literally translated, means "concentration." It is used symbolically by the Hindu mystic to signify concentration or union with a Supreme Being. According to the fourth chapter of the Bhagavad Gita, many "adepts," in order to be entirely freed from the distraction of bodily sensations, even "sacrifice the sense of hearing and the other senses in the fires of restraint." Others, "by abstaining from food, sacrifice life in their life."

There is no difference in principle between these practices and the self-flagellations of the early monks, the Master's forty-day fast in the wilderness, and the asceticism of Simeon Stylites, who passed his life on top of a pillar. *All* these procedures must be looked upon as *devices* intended to facilitate mental concentration.

Think, now, of the advantage that you possess over other exponents of the art of concentration. You have learned the exact truth in regard to mental operations and processes. You have taken a vast amount of pains in doing so. But now that it comes time for you to apply these principles by devising easy ways for practicing concentration with a view to attaining specific results, you do not have to go groping about in the darkness of occultism and mystery.

You know the elements with which you have to deal.

You know them as realities, as demonstrable truths of modern science.

And when you come to make use of these devices, you will not question their efficacy. You will have no doubts as to your success. You will be inspired with *the faith that is born of knowledge,* as distinguished from the faith that is artificially created by mystic formulas and priestly authority.

The faith that *knows* was the faith of the Son of God. Jesus knew the power of the human spirit. He *knew* how to heal the sick, how to feed the multitude with but a single loaf, how to confer the peace "that passeth understanding." This was the secret of his perfect power.

Yet even Jesus required certain conditions for the "demonstration" of his powers. Even Jesus was unable to perform miracles among the people of Nazareth because of their *"unbelief."* And it was Jesus who, when he had healed a certain sick man, uttered these words of deep scientific significance— "Thy *faith* hath made thee whole."

Faith, belief in the attainment of a desired end, is as essential to success scientifically sought as sought in any other way, because, as you have seen, it sets in motion actual forces.

But scientific method possesses four exclusive advantages. *First, the faith it demands is a faith that all may acquire, because it is a faith that reasoning will create, not destroy; second, it is a faith that is perfect, because based on judgment; third, it is a faith that is lasting because truth is immutable; fourth, it is a faith that you may deliberately and scientifically acquire, because you now know that faith in a given idea means nothing more nor less than the dominance of that idea in consciousness.*

So, then, you can achieve nothing without faith—faith in the ideals on which your attention dwells.

And through faith and ideals, and your *consecration of them*, and your *concentration upon them*, lies the way for you to acquire inner control, to escape wasteful moods and emotions, to master your energies, to become *efficient* in the highest sense and to the last degree.[2]

You now have Dr. Hilton's version of concentration. I have found his explanations practical and entirely in harmony with my own discoveries.

How to Select Your Life's Work

Vocational guidance has not yet become a universally accepted science, but this does not preclude a person from using common sense in selecting a vocation. The trouble is, too many people act on a "hunch." If you are engaged in work in which you are not succeeding, take inventory of yourself and see if you cannot locate the trouble. The chances are that you can. Just apply common sense in selecting your life's work. You may not be able to analyze yourself as well as a man who has had many years of experience; therefore, if you have any doubts, place yourself in the hands of someone who is experienced in analyzing men. He will undoubtedly see your weak spots more quickly than you could. Few of us can be our own best critics because we are inclined to overlook our weaknesses or place too little importance on them.

There are but few, if any, ironclad rules to follow in the selection of a vocation that would apply in every case. Probably these come as near as being applicable in all cases as is possible. *Be sure you love the vocation you adopt! Be sure you are enthusiastic about it and that you intend to stick with it! Be sure you are prepared, educationally, for the work you select! Be sure the vocation is one in which you render a service that is beneficial to humanity! Be sure the work is permanent! Be sure that it is work that will not impair your health!*

How to Get What You Want

We come to the last, and probably the most important, subject of all—namely, "How to Get What You Want." It is through the discussion of this subject that I shall try to show you how to make application of the principles covered up to this point. Selecting the right vocation would mean nothing to you unless you knew how to develop that vocation through the proper use of the principles herein set out and explained. I am writing at length on this subject because the research that I have done in my work as a personal analyst has shown me how sadly lacking the average person is in the knowledge concerning the principles that I shall mention. Without a fair understanding of these principles, what I have written up to this point would be practically useless.

The most stupendous problem confronting the human race today is the question "How can I get what I want?"

In the business office, on the streetcars, in the home, in the city, and on the farm, in America and all over the world, wherever men and women congregate, the conversation drifts to this great subject. Probably the most vitally important knowledge that I have gained from my research as an analyst is this law of nature of which I shall write and through the application of which *you can get whatever you want*.

Obviously there are more ways than one to get what we want, but it is just as obvious to the well-balanced, thinking person that there is only one correct way, and my purpose is to point out this correct way in the simplest words at my command.

Who am I that I should set myself up as an authority on such a momentous question?

I answer that I am only one of the many thousands who have discovered this principle of which I am writing by first having tried out its opposite in the crucible of life and finding it wanting. I am only one of the thousands who have wrested this secret from the great mass of human effort that we call "experience," most of which was for many years misdirected and out of harmony with the purpose of life.

I am only relating that which thousands of others have learned at a most appalling cost, in heartaches and disappointments—relating it with the hope that your pathway in seeking that which you want may be a little smoother, a little more pleasant, as a result of what I have written in my humble way.

I am positive that the principle—nay, let me call it the *law* of nature—with which I shall acquaint you is scientifically correct and that it offers the only desirable route to that which you want.

The reason I am so sure of this is the fact that for more than fifteen years I exerted every effort at my command to deny this principle and to reach my desired goal without making use of it.

So this is why I have presumed to present my viewpoint. In presenting it, I am doing it neither for profit nor for the purpose of trying to entertain you. I am presenting it for your use for the sole reason that I am only happy and successful in proportion to the extent that I help others become happy and successful.

In calling your attention to this simple law, let me hasten to explain that I lay no claim to its original discovery.

This law is as available to one person as it is to another, and furthermore, it has been available to us all ever since the world began. I make this explanation so you will not accuse me, in the silence of your heart, of the unpardonable act of trying to clothe a great law of nature in occultism, or of an attempt to present this principle as a "manmade" product.

Electricity has given the world a problem to contend with for ages. It was and still is a force—an energy of which we know comparatively little. At one stage of the world's evolution we shrank away from the lightning in the clouds and believed it was sort of evidence of God's wrath toward ignorant humanity.

But Franklin was no skeptic! Neither was he a fanatic, and being open-minded, a thinker and a student of nature, he sent up his kite with a key tied to it and thus got into communication with that energy that most other people of his time didn't understand and were afraid of.

Then came Edison, and by discovering some of nature's laws and adapting himself to them he harnessed electricity and made it light our houses, turn our machinery, and pull our trains. Edison didn't invent electricity—he merely discovered how to make use of a law which anyone before him could have made use of had he adapted himself to it.

And so it is with this law of nature, through the operation of which you can get that which you want.

In explaining this law, I shall show you how to get what you want through its use, but there is one thing I cannot tell you—and that is *what to want*!

Now as to this great principle, let me quote the following from one of the world's leading authorities, a man who probably discovered the principle just as I did—by and through an exhaustive research in life's laboratory:

> *There is a thinking stuff from which all things are made and which, in its original state, permeates, penetrates, and fills the interspaces of the universe.*
>
> *A thought, in this substance, produces the thing that is imaged by the thought.*

Man can form things in his thought, and, by impressing his thought upon formless substance, can cause the thing he thinks about to be created.

In order to do this...he must form a clear mental picture of the things he wants, and do, with faith and purpose, all that can be done each day, doing each separate thing in an efficient manner.[3]

"As a man thinketh in his heart, so is he."

The words quoted above state the entire principle about which I am writing. Or, stated in another familiar quotation in the words of the world's greatest psychologist:

"Whatsoever ye soweth, that shall ye also reap."

If there is the slightest doubt in your mind that something must first be created in your mind before it can be created elsewhere, I implore you to dismiss that thought before you are caught and permanently held in that great maelstrom of skepticism, doubt, and lack of faith in the simple laws of nature, which have enmeshed so many human beings who fail to get what they want.

I say that to those who "fail to get *what they want*," but upon reflection, I seriously doubt that such a thing is possible as one failing to get what one *really wants*!

Right here is a fine line to be drawn and kept in mind; namely, there is a great deal of difference between merely *wishing* for a thing and *wanting* it with all your heart and soul, wanting it so much that you make up your mind that *you are going* to get it, no matter what effort may be necessary, *and then proceed to get it*!

> *You will get what you think about most intensely.*

Right here is the danger point—the place where the average person loses contact with and understanding of this great law. The truth of the matter is that you are either consciously or unconsciously getting *that which you think about most intensely.* That is something you will do well to remember!

I consider this point so important that I feel it my duty to digress from my subject for just a moment while I explain that you are reading, not the words that have fallen from the pencil of a religious fanatic, but the words of a fairly well-balanced businessman—a man who has tasted rather liberally of both poverty and riches, a man who has probably gone through just such experiences as you yourself have faced!

I make this explanation for the reason that fifteen of my twenty years of business experience were failures, not because I couldn't avail myself of the information that I am passing on to you, but because I looked upon all attempts to expound this principle as emanating from impractical, distorted, and more or less unbalanced minds.

I now know better! And the pity of it all is that I have lost fifteen years—probably one-fifth of my entire allotment on this earth—before discovering my mistake.

I say to you without qualifications that you will be forced to accept the truth of this simple law before you can expediently attain any desirable position in life; therefore,

I trust that I can help you extricate yourself from the mass of entangling thoughts that may now be holding you away from the desirable things of life.

This message, then, is just a simple message from a plain businessman who has "found himself" and who not only knows that he has found himself, but who knows exactly *how* he found himself and desires to point out the way to you.

Now before we proceed with the subject, let's again state this principle or law in nature in plain, concrete words that cannot be misunderstood:

Everything that we create in physical form must first be created in thought! Thoughts that we concentrate our minds upon will, in time, reproduce themselves in physical form. We grow to resemble the thoughts which we dwell upon most.

That is the principle, stated in the simplest words at my command. Now let us apply the principle and see how it worked out in at least one authentic, concrete case, when it was consciously made use of. (We are always making use of this principle, but most of the time we use it unconsciously and through its operations defeat our own purpose.)

The value to you of this principle will depend largely upon whether you learn to use it consciously, in an organized way, or unconsciously, without understanding it.

Remember, the only thing lightning ever did before it was harnessed was to frighten people, and now and then, kill someone.

It is the same with the principles of which I am writing—they may act as a boomerang to destroy you unless you harness them and apply them *consciously* and in an organized manner.

The concrete example that I shall make use of is this (and I use it because I know it to be authentic):

For nearly a score of years a very close personal friend of mine wanted to accumulate money, a desire that I presume you also have had at times.

I say he "wanted" money, but in reality I believe he merely "wished" for it, because he gave but little thought as to what he would give in return or as to just how he would proceed in getting money. He was trying to reap a harvest of money without sowing a crop of useful service to humanity; therefore, he was out of harmony with nature's law—"Whatsoever ye soweth, that shall ye also reap."

At about the end of the eighteenth of those twenty years he came to an understanding of this principle, and during the last two of the twenty years he has created not only part of the money he desired, but he has discovered the greatest of all discoveries—namely, *how to be happy!* He wanted to get money so he might be happy and help to make others happy, but his thoughts were centered on the *effect*; and he thereby overlooked the *cause* through which to create that *effect*.

During those eighteen years he devoted most of his time to thinking and creating means through which to get possession of what others had already created, and instead of succeeding, his thoughts came back like a boomerang and defeated his purpose!

Why? Because he had been concentrating his entire mind on defeating others, and in doing so he created *defeat*, but for himself.

"As a man thinketh in his heart, so is he."

He thought of defeat and was *defeated*! He made the wrong use of auto-suggestion because he didn't understand it.

Auto-suggestion is a wonderful power that you are using either consciously or unconsciously in getting what you want, but I warn you that it is a power that may bring about your downfall if you make the wrong use of it.

I said I would tell you how to get what you want, but the responsibility of deciding what you want must rest upon your shoulders. Proceed in this way: when you have made your decision, *create a clear outline of the thing you have decided to do or the person you have decided to be, write out a description of it, and memorize this description.*

After you have memorized it, you must make use of the power of auto-suggestion and affirm to yourself and to others, if you choose, that you are going to create or acquire the thing you have decided upon. Make this affirmation at least a dozen times a day, preferably by stating in forceful words addressed, if necessary, to an imaginary person.

Now, let me caution you again to be very careful to see that you do not make the mistake of choosing to create or acquire that which you will not desire after you get it. This principle does not discriminate. *It brings you what you order!*

For many years I desired to become a successful writer!

A writer on what subject?

Oh, any old subject—it made no difference so long as I could see my name in print as an author.

It hadn't occurred to me until recent years that writing is but the outward expression of inward feelings, and that before anything worth reading can come out, something worth reading must "go in" and be recast from the crucible of the human heart.

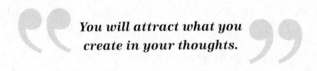

You will attract what you create in your thoughts.

I make this unqualified statement: that you can attract to you—nay, that you *will* attract to you—the very things, or the very station in life, that you create in your thoughts.

Choose wisely, then, the material that goes into those thoughts. Go a step further and organize your thoughts by drawing a very clear and definite mental picture of the thing you wish to acquire or of the person you wish to be, and then concentrate on that picture until you transform it into a physical reality. You now understand the principle of concentration; therefore, make use of it!

Just in proportion to the extent that your mental picture is clear and complete will your material realization of it be clear and complete.

Remember, then, that to merely wish for a thing now and then is neither clear nor complete. Go a step further, and through the power of *strong* desire paint a picture of what you want that is so definite and clear that none—particularly yourself—can mistake it.

This principle applies to the accumulation of every material thing on earth and to the creation of every state of mind. Through its use we can be happy or unhappy, prosperous or poor, just as we choose.

Every principle that I have herein recommended has been tried out and proven practical and scientifically correct. Through the students of the George Washington Institute I have seen these principles work remarkable results, *in some cases almost instantly*. In fact, the principles which I have herein mentioned form the very warp and woof of what we term the "idealistic" portion of the course in "Advertising and Salesmanship" taught by the Institute—that is, that portion of the course through which we develop in the student a magnetic and pleasing personality, without which a mastery of the mere technique or mechanics of advertising would be almost useless.

It is no secret among those who are familiar with the policy under which the George Washington Institute is conducted that its worldwide popularity is due entirely to the fact that it has applied from the beginning the principle herein mentioned. There really is no mystery in the fact that within the short period of one year, the George Washington Institute, through the application of these principles, and without a dollar in capital to start with, created a business that has almost encircled the earth—a business that has accomplished more in a year than any other correspondence school ever accomplished in five years during the "beginning" stage.

This is not a "boast" for the George Washington Institute—the institute doesn't need it—but merely another concrete proof that these principles are commercially sound!

A few years ago I tried in vain to get one of the largest correspondence schools in Chicago to teach at least one of these vitally fundamental principles, but its owners declined my offer with the statement that these principles were "too idealistic for our use." This school evidently believed that a part of my plans was not "too idealistic," however, for it stole bodily my idea.

I mention this incident, not in a spirit of vindictiveness, but only for the purpose of making the point that the wrong application of a correct principle will not succeed, neither will it prove that principle to be impractical or incorrect, and also to make the point that success cannot be attained by merely applying a part of one or more of these principles.

No, I feel no animosity toward the owners of the school because they tried to steal my plans. To do so would be the equivalent of permitting these misguided gentlemen *to pull me down to their level*, and in that event I would be directly violating one of the most important of the principles I have mentioned.

If a man steals your idea, let him alone with it, for he will soon hang himself with it. Spend no time hating such a man because you are damaging yourself and not him.

> *If a man steals your idea, let him alone with it, for he will soon hang himself with it.*

Remember that your thoughts are building your "personality"; therefore, be careful as to what sort of thoughts go into that building.

The last thought that I shall leave with you is this: the degree of the "bigness" or "littleness" to which a person has risen may be very accurately determined by ascertaining the extent to which that person can *forgive* and *forget* the wrongs which have been heaped upon him.

Show me a person who has enough self-control to refrain from joining the chorus when he hears someone who has done him injustice being "picked to pieces" by his gossiping neighbors, and there I will show you a person who has made at least the first step toward *greatness*.

Forbear and *forgive—forget forever*—if you would be considerate of *your own* welfare and happiness.

Remember the words of the world's greatest philosopher: "If any among ye is without sin let him cast the first stone."

An attractive and magnetic personality is essential for success in any worthwhile undertaking. If the principles that I have mentioned are correct, a person can be neither attractive nor magnetic as long as he harbors hatred in his heart.

On November 11, 1918, Armistice Day ending World War I, Napoleon Hill wrote, "The slaughter has ceased and reason is about to reclaim civilization once more."

Hill remarked on this date that he was in search of one of his own principles of success: a Definite Major Purpose. Hill sat down at his typewriter and began to do the only thing he knew how to do really well: he began writing. He later remarked, "I just wrote whatever came into my mind." Hill said this was the beginning of the most important turning point of his life. Hill said that "from the war a new idealism will come—an idealism that will be based on the Golden Rule philosophy; an idealism that will guide us, not to see how much we can 'do our fellow man for' but how much we can do for him, that will ameliorate his hardships and make him happier as he tarries by the wayside of life. To get this philosophy to the public and into the hearts of those that need it, I shall publish a magazine to be called *Hill's Golden Rule*."

Within a week of writing his first essay, Hill took it to George Williams, a Chicago printer whom he knew through his work in the White House on wartime propaganda material.

Hill's Golden Rule Magazine was an outlet for something that had been building inside of him since he was a young lad. When his stepmother had traded his gun for a typewriter, he had been thrilled to turn out news stories for local papers. It was said of Hill that when he had no worthy news, he would invent some.

Perhaps it was because of his attendance at the Three Forks Primitive Baptist Church, of which his father was one of the founders, that he understood the ability of speakers to electrify large crowds of followers. Here Hill learned how he might obtain the fame of which his stepmother had told him he was capable when he was just thirteen years old. As a result of this influence, Hill's writings blend words from the Bible with lessons of Carnegie, Ford, and other modern-day success stories that he gathered from his interviews.

For his first issue of *Napoleon Hill's Golden Rule Magazine*, Hill produced forty-eight pages written and edited entirely by him. The printed copy was delivered to newsstands in January 1919.

Hill had no money to back the magazine publication, making it even less likely to succeed—yet it did. The first issue was so popular that it went through three print runs.

With the success of *Napoleon Hill's Golden Rule Magazine,* Hill was increasingly sought after for personal appearances. He had requests from large groups, and he began setting a one hundred-dollar speaking fee.

On one speaking assignment in Davenport, Iowa, where he was to lecture to two thousand students, Hill refused his usual one hundred-dollar speaking fee and was rewarded with six thousand dollars in subscriptions.

In the same year, Hill told of an invite from George S. Parker of the Parker Pen Company in Janesville, Wisconsin. According to Hill, upon his arrival, Parker took Hill's hand, placed his around Hill's shoulder, and said, "I invited you up here so I could see for myself if you were sincere in your belief in the Golden Rule. Now that I've looked into your heart I have only this to say—you'll never know, as long as you live, the tremendous amount of good you are doing through your magazine."

Hill admired others who had overcome adversity, and one of his first studies was of Samuel Smiles, who in 1859 wrote *Self-Help*, one of the first books in the personal-development genre. For most of the people about whom Hill wrote, it took several years for them to succeed at their endeavors. One of his examples was Josiah Wedgwood, who perfected the process of making china. He founded his company on May 1, 1759, and it is still in business today. "Wedgwood china," as it is now called, is desired by people around the globe.

Hill spent his life studying why people succeed, but he dedicated time to understanding why people fail. Edward Bok, publisher of the acclaimed *Ladies' Home Journal*, was another man whose life Hill examined because he overcame adversity to ultimately succeed. Bok wrote to Hill, and that letter formed the basis of one of Hill's lectures—"The Man Who Has Had No Chance"—for his students at the George Washington Institute. The Edward Bok story is an example of how Hill used others' experiences to learn from defeat and overcome adversity.

—DON GREEN

The Man Who Has Had No Chance

by
Napoleon Hill

In my vocational work I get hundreds of letters from men who say, "I never had a chance!" Many of them complain of the hard times they have had in getting along, of their failures, handicaps, and drawbacks. Poor fellows, they don't know how well off they are. They have not learned that most seeming adversities are, in reality, blessings in disguise. I never hear of a man who has gone through the mill of experience rather roughly that I don't say, "Congratulations!"

A few years ago my younger brother graduated from law school. He paid his own way through school. He worked all day and went to school at night. On his graduation day I sent him this simple little note:

Boy, this is a big day for you! It is a big day because you are now ready to begin learning law. Four years in law school has laid a fairly good foundation on which to build a permanent legal structure. You have had no easy time during these four years. I can testify to that from my own experience. My sincerest wish is that during the next four years you may complete the seasoning process and become a real lawyer. I sincerely trust you will not be successful financially to begin with. If you are, it will deprive you of much that you need. Before you can appreciate the responsibility which you are assuming in acting as legal advisor for men and women in all walks of life you must experience much of the bitter side of life. So, during the next four years (and God grant that you may not need more time than this) I trust you may know what it is to go hungry.

I trust that you may taste of that necessary experience through which most great men have undergone. Boy, you'll need this baptism of fire before you are ready to serve the world in the profession that you have selected. While others are wishing you success with little effort, I am wishing you success *with great effort*! You will not get another such note as this; of that I am reasonably sure. I leave it to you, however, as to who has the better knowledge of what you will need to succeed—your humble servant, the writer, or those who are showering you with congratulations.

This may seem like a rather heartless letter to write to one's own brother; at least it may seem so to those who have not yet learned the value of a hard time. But to those who have gone through this valuable experience of fighting for an existence I need make no apologies for my letter to my brother. They will understand!

I have not had what you would call an "easy time," but my experience has not been as severe as that of some others. For this reason I will not enter into the details. Instead of my own story I shall relate one that is more suited to my point. When I began writing this lecture I called to mind some of the men of my acquaintance who had started at the bottom and landed at the top via the hard-experience route. Among them was Mr. Edward W. Bok, editor of one of the world's greatest magazines, the *Ladies' Home Journal*. I requested Mr. Bok's story. Here it is, just as he sent it to me. And if there are no tears in your eyes when you are through, you may pronounce yourself to be short of emotional feeling.

Why I Believe in Poverty as the Richest Experience that Can Come to a Boy

I make my living trying to edit the *Ladies' Home Journal*. And because the public has been most generous in its acceptance of that periodical, a share of that success has logically come to me. Hence a number of my very good readers cherish an opinion that often I have been tempted to correct, a temptation to which I now yield. My correspondents express the conviction variously, but this extract from a letter is a fair sample:

"It is all very easy for you to preach economy to us when you do not know the necessity of it—to tell us how, as, for example, in my own case, we must live within my husband's income of eight hundred dollars a year, when you have never known what it is to live on less than thousands. Has it ever occurred to you, born with the proverbial silver spoon in your mouth, that theoretical writing is pretty cold and futile compared to the actual hand-to-mouth struggle that so many of us live day by day and year in and year out, an experience that you know not of?"

"An experience that you know not of"!

Now, how far do the facts square with this statement?

Whether or not I was born with the proverbial silver spoon in my mouth I cannot say. It is true that I was born of well-to-do parents. But when I was six years old, my father lost all his means and faced life at forty-five, in a strange country, without even necessaries. There are men and their wives who know what that means—for a man to try to "come back" at forty-five, and in a strange country!

I had the handicap of not knowing one word of the English language. I went to a public school and learned what I could. And sparse morsels they were! The boys were cruel, as boys are. The teachers were impatient, as tired teachers are.

My father could not find his place in the world. My mother, who had always had servants at her beck and call, faced the problems of housekeeping that she had never learned nor been taught.

And there was no money.

So, after school hours, my brother and I went home, but not to play. After-school hours meant time for us to help a mother who daily grew frailer under the burdens that she could not carry. Not for days but for years, we two boys got up in the gray, cold winter dawn, when the bed feels so snug and warm to growing boys, and we sifted the cold ashes of the day-before's fire for a stray lump or two of unburned coal, and with what we had or could find we made the fire and warmed up the room. Then, we set the table for the scant breakfast, went to school, and directly after school we washed the dishes and swept and scrubbed the floors. Living in a three-family tenement, each third week meant that we scrubbed the entire three flights of stairs from the third story to the first, as well as the door-steps and the sidewalk outside. The latter work was the hardest; for we did it on Saturdays, with the boys of the neighborhood looking on none too kindly, so we did it to the echo of the crack of the ball and bat on the adjoining lot!

In the evening when the other boys could sit by the lamp or study their lessons, we two boys went out with a basket and picked up wood and coal in the adjoining lots, or went after the dozen or so pieces of coal left from the ton of coal put in that afternoon by one of the neighbors, with the spot hungrily fixed in mind by one of us during the day, hoping that the man who carried in the coal might not be too careful in picking up the stray lumps!

An experience that you know not of! Don't I?

At ten years of age I got my first job: washing the windows of a baker's shop at fifty cents a week. In a week or two I was allowed to sell bread and cakes behind the counter after school hours for a dollar a week—handing out freshly baked cakes and warm, delicious-smelling bread, when scarcely a crumb had passed my mouth that day!

Then on Saturday mornings I served a route for a weekly paper and sold my remaining stock on the street. It meant from sixty to seventy cents for that day's work.

I lived in Brooklyn, New York, and the chief means of transportation to Coney Island at that time was the horse car. Near where we lived, the cars would stop to water the horses, the men would jump out and get a drink of water, but the women had no means of quenching their thirst. Seeing this lack I got a pail, filled it with water and a bit of ice, and with a glass, jumped on each car Saturday after-noon and all day Sunday, and sold my wares at a cent a glass. And when competition came, as it did very quickly when other boys saw that a Sunday's work meant two or three dollars, I squeezed a lemon or two in my pail, my liquid became "lemonade" and my price two cents a glass, and Sunday meant five dollars to me.

Then, in turn I became a reporter during evenings, an office boy daytimes, and learned stenography at midnight.

My correspondent says she supports her family of husband and child on eight hundred dollars a year and says I have never known what that means. I supported a family of three on six dollars and twenty-five cents a week—less than one-half of her yearly income. When my brother and I, combined, brought in eight hundred dollars a year, we felt rich!

I have for the first time gone into these details in print so that you may know, at firsthand, that the editor of the *Ladies' Home Journal* is not a theorist when he writes or prints articles that seek to preach economy or that reflect a hand-to-hand struggle on a small or an invisible income. There is not a single step, not an inch on the road of direct poverty that I do not know or have not experienced. And, having experienced every thought, every feeling, and every hardship that came to those who travel that road, I say today that I rejoice with every boy who is going through the same experience.

Nor am I discounting or forgetting one single pang of the keen hardships that such a struggle means. I would not today exchange my years of the keenest hardship that a boy can know or pass through for any single experience that could have come to me. I know what it means, not to earn a dollar, but to earn two cents. I know the value of money as I could have learned it or known it in no other way. I could have been trained for my life's work no surer way. I could not have arrived at a truer understanding of what it means to face a day without a penny in hand, not a loaf of bread in the cupboard, not a piece of kindling wood for the fire—with nothing to eat, and then a boy with the hunger of nine and ten, with a mother frail and discouraged!

An experience that you know not of! Don't I?

And yet I rejoice in the experience, and I repeat, I envy every boy who is in that condition and going through it. But—and here is the pivot of my strong belief in poverty as an undisguised blessing to a boy—I believe in poverty as a condition to experience, to go through, and then to get out of, not as a condition to stay in. "That's all very well," some will say. "Easy enough to say, but how can you get out of it?" No one can definitely tell another that. No one told me. No two persons can find the same way out. Each must find his way for himself. That depends on the boy. I was determined to get out of poverty because my mother was not born in it, could not stand it, and did not belong in it. This gave me the first essential: a purpose.

Then I backed up the purpose with effort and will-ingness to work and to work at anything that came my way, no matter what it was, so long as it meant "the way out." I did not pick and choose; I took what came, and I did it in the best way I knew how. And when I didn't like what I was doing, I still did it well while I was doing it, but I saw to it that I didn't do it any longer than I had to do it. I used every rung in the ladder as a rung to the above one. It meant effort, but out of the effort and the work came the experience; the up-building, the development; the capacity to understand and sympathize; the greatest heritage that can come to a boy. And nothing in the world can give that to a boy, so that it will burn into him, as will poverty.

That is why I believe so strongly in poverty, the greatest blessing in the way of the deepest and fullest experience that can come to a boy. But, as I repeat: always as a condition to work out of, not to stay in.

You have read the story of a man "who had no chance." And you envy that man in his position, don't you? I do! Edward Bok has made good in a big way. He has profited by his early adversities. Truly, they were blessings in dis-guise! I love to read that story of Mr. Bok's early struggles. I have read it until I can repeat it by heart. It gives me renewed courage and determination. It helps my tired legs to support me when they might otherwise let me fall by the wayside. It makes me unsheathe my sword and fight my seeming adversities like they were demons from hell! It dispels discouragement and lights my pathway through life. It makes me love the world more; it makes me a better citizen. I trust that Mr. Bok's simple little story will reach and quicken the hearts of a million readers.

> *Adversities make me love the world more; it makes me a better citizen.*

I know the story of another man that you will want to hear about, Reddy Johnson. He too is a big, successful businessman now, and like Mr. Bok, he began right down at the bottom. Not so many years ago, he was a helper in a machine shop at wages of $1.60 a day. Now he owns the whole works and a great deal more besides. I want you to know the story of *how he sold his services*! In this story by an unknown author, you will have the whole crux of my philosophy on this subject, so here it is:

> "There's a lot of talk about success in life printed nowadays; some of it is pretty good, and I suppose it does much good. A lot of you fellows need considerable trimming anyway. But, to my mind, they don't any of them reach down to the root of the matter like my first lesson did. You fellows talk about the scarcity of good men, tell how you are driven to secure foremen that know more than the men they've got to boss, how scarce superintendents are, how good salesmen are worth their weight in gold, and all that sort of thing. I suppose

it encourages some who are already on the right path so that they'll keep on improving themselves a little, but it doesn't go to the root of the matter. It doesn't start a crop of lively youngsters who will all be fit to take the places of us fellows with white hair—or with no hair, like me.

"Now, I ain't worrying any on that score, I've got a lively crop of youngsters in training back at the works, and I've given some of them away, or rather, loaned 'em, and I'll get 'em again just as soon as they have gotten a little riper. You can't make a salesman or foreman out of every man you pick up, but you can make good ones out of a surprisingly large proportion of the boys of today if you start 'em right, give 'em the proper mental training and lots of practice like I got."

"Give us the recipe, uncle," said the redheaded jewelry drummer. "I'm needing more salary myself, and I'm looking for points."

"Away back in—well, never mind, it's a good while ago—I was a redheaded kid in a machine shop, and I guess I was pretty bumptious. I was about eighteen and had nearly served my time and wanted a foremanship worse than I wanted anything else in the world. You laugh at my wanting to be a foreman before I'd finished my time, but if the truth was known, that's about the ideal of every cub at that age. They don't say so—I didn't then—but that's about it, and it's a good, legitimate ambition.

"We had a traveler named Van who sold about all the product of the shop, and it was currently reported that he had graduated from the shop and was getting three thousand a year and doing just as he pleased. Every time he came in from the road he would come out in the shop, give cigars to the foreman and super, and shake hands with every man and boy in the shop. Then he would go around with the old man discussing the work and looking after the details of his orders, and what he said always went with the old man. You'd think that he owned the shop and the old man was the super, if you didn't know. Well, I looked on Van as a prince. When I got tired of imagining myself as a foreman I would sometimes wonder if I would ever earn as much as Van—three thousand dollars a year! And I was getting $1.60 a day. Three thousand dollars was untold wealth to me.

"One morning I was in a fearful temper, discontented with myself and the world; some of the men had sprung some old gags that morning and I had bit on all of them. Naturally that hadn't helped any. Van came up behind me and blew a cloud of smoke, making me cough. I picked up a wrench, but when I saw it was Van I dropped it and laughed; nobody could get mad at Van.

"'Well, Reddy,' he said, 'when are you going to be foreman?' Then he sat down and drew me out. Finally he said: 'You can be foreman, either of this place or some other, just as soon as you've had sufficient practice in bossing men. Everybody wants foremen and superintendents and salesmen, and all you've got to do is to start in and practice as you did on the lathe and planer.'

"'How can I practice? I'm only a cub here; everybody tells me what to do and I've got to do it. They can practice on me all right; most of them are doing it good and plenty. How am I going to get anyone to practice on?'

"'Well, Reddy, there's one man whom you can practice on; that's Johnson.'

"'Me?'

"'No, not you, but Johnson. Every man has two pretty distinct personalities in the one body. One is energetic, ambitious, likes to do right and get along—that's you. The other is careless, shiftless, lazy, and fond of a good time—that's Johnson. Now, what you've got to do is to learn to boss Johnson, and you'll find it will take a lot of practice. When you get so that you can boss Johnson successfully—keep him right up to the mark all the time and keep him good-natured about it—then, and not until then, you'll have the skill and practice to boss more than one man. Now, there's the man for you to practice on. Will you do it? Shake! I feel sorry for Johnson, for he'll have to stand it. I'm going to be around here for a week and I'll start you right. I'll tell you what to do and you can tell Johnson, just as the old man gives orders to the super and you get them from the super.

That completes the chain and makes it a working agreement.'

"Well, I was boy enough so that the idea tickled me. Van would come around and say, 'Reddy, tell Johnson to do this, and keep after him; see that he does it.'

"In the course of a week I began to like the game. I also found out a lot of things I had never suspected. As Reddy, the foreman, I used to jack myself up as Johnson, the workman, and according to Reddy, Johnson was a good deal of a slob. Van went on the road and I kept after Johnson night and day. I ordered him to bed and I ordered him up. I checked up on his work and I made him study. As Reddy, the foreman, I thought less of myself as Johnson, the workman, until my opinion of Johnson was at a pretty low ebb. I noticed that the old man was watching me a good deal, and I began to be afraid that Johnson would get fired, so Reddy drove Johnson harder than ever.

Bossing Johnson

"One night I went to a show, and before the curtain rose I heard two people talking in front of me. One had been away, and he said: 'How's Reddy Johnson doing?' 'Fine,' said the other; 'he's assistant foreman at the shops now, in charge of the erecting, with from three to ten men under him all the time.'

"I heard no more of the play. Was I foreman? When did I become foreman? How long had I been foreman? When the new wing was put up six months before, I was put to work in it with some helpers and my wages had been raised. Yes, I had been foreman for six months and was so busy bossing Johnson I hadn't noticed it. Had to have outsiders tell me about it!

"Six months later I was offered a superintendency of another factory at about double the wages, and the firm advised me to take it, saying that I could come back if I didn't make good. That aroused all the fight in me, and I made good. I think every redheaded man is sensitive to insinuations.

"I kept on bossing Johnson until I made a salesman out of him. Now I own some works myself. I am as far ahead of Van's three thousand dollars a year as I was behind it when I started. I haven't had a salary in twenty years. In my own works I have gotten a number of kids that have started to practice on themselves till they are able to hold a foreman's job, and there are some others scattered around getting experience that I'll get back when I want them. The scheme is working as well with them as it did with me. You see, it's fundamental. It starts the boy right and gives him the idea of self-control from the beginning. That's all that makes the difference between the proprietor and the employee: one can boss himself; the other can't. It's an old idea. The Bible says, 'He that is a master of himself is greater than he that taketh a city.' I'm a Democrat and can't quote scripture, but it's something to that effect.

"Now, my redheaded friend, you said you wanted a raise in salary. Why not start now to get ready for the time when you won't need a salary—won't accept it? I tell you, boys, before you can get off a salary you've got to boss Johnson—all the time, night and day."

The old man went out, and for a long ten minutes nobody said anything. They just sat there and thought it over.

Now, if you, my reader, have not learned how to "boss Johnson," get busy immediately. And when you shall have made a good job of it, straighten up, look around about you and you will discover that you have become foreman of the works.

Every once in a while I get a letter from some earnest, well-meaning fellow who complains that he is not getting along very well because he didn't have a chance to go to college. When I receive one of these complaints, I cannot help recalling the cases of four young men whom I know to be succeeding yet who didn't have the advantage of college training. One of these young men was formerly my private secretary. He began working for me while I was advertising manager for a western corporation. He started in at a salary of seventy-five dollars a month. He was just out of business college and he was not even a good stenographer. He had never been to high school. In fact, he had never completed the grade school work. Six months later he became my assistant at $150 a month, and when I resigned, he stepped into my position—at a big salary.

Only this last Christmas I had letters from three of these boys. They were in business college at the same time I was. One of them is advertising manager of one of New York's big department stores at a salary of ten thousand dollars a year, one is assistant to a high official of the United States Steel Corporation at a salary of six thousand dollars a year, and the other one is secretary of one of the largest automobile concerns in the country at a salary of eight thousand dollars a year. We all began the same year, in the same business college; we all had about the same previous educational advantages, which were none too great at best. We all started out as stenographers and bookkeepers.

I have never been able to see that any of these boys suffered very much on account of not having gone to college. They might have been doing better now had they gone to college, and again they might not have been doing as well, for college men usually are unwilling to begin with such a humble position as that of stenographer.

I read a corking good article on the subject of the relationship of education to success, which appeared in *The Fra* some months ago. It was written by Mr. C. A. Munn, editor of *The Scientific American*, and it is worth passing on, so here it is:

> While the value of a higher education is in our day fairly generally appreciated, there are not wanting voices that ask: "What gain does this education bring to the individual? Is it not true that we see men of little or no schooling winning in the race over others who have had every opportunity that institutions of learning can offer? Nay, more, are

there not numberless instances of men to whom their very education has been a stumbling-block, whom it has made blind to opportunities recognized and seized upon by their more alert brothers of less schooling, and perhaps more common-sense? Do we not see educated men following after dreams and visions, while their more practical, though less erudite, fellows are gathering a material harvest?" In brief, "Is education on the whole conducive of success?"

If by education were meant an ideal education, we should hardly hesitate to answer with an emphatic "Yes." Insofar, however, as actual education departs from the ideal, there will, of course, be instances in which it fails to lead to the highest degree of success that might have been attained with a given raw material under prescribed circumstances.

> *We must endeavor to see things in their true perspective.*

To cast a sound judgment on this question, we must put away the personal point of view, whether centered about our own self or about some other specific individual, in whom perhaps we are personally interested. We must endeavor to see things in their true perspective.

To the educator, whose function it is to assist in molding the raw material of this generation, and who, from the nature of this activity, is brought to view classes of individuals collectively, this point of view must be perfectly familiar. Is it not an obvious sign of some imperfection in the methods or materials with which he has worked, if this or that individual of his charge in later years accumulates personal profits at the expense of his fellows without due compensation? Yet, so long as he keeps within the law and accepted custom, he may do this and be reckoned by many a "success," because they take only a personal survey of the situation and lose sight of the interests of the community.

While flagrant breaches of the principles implied above are recognized by all as criminal, it is far from being generally understood that every "success," which is success only from a personal standpoint, is in fact a failure.

But some may say, barring exceptional cases, is not the world's estimate of the value of a man a very fair approximation to the truth? To this the reply seems to be, that the world's estimate of a man's services is indeed, broadly speaking, a fair approximation to the truth, in most cases, but we are not here concerned with the case that represents the rule—there seems to be a fairly general agreement that, as a rule, a higher education is an aid toward success; the cases which are of interest in our present discussion are the exceptional cases, in which apparently the result of education has been to handicap the individual. Is not the explanation of at least some of these cases to be found in the disparity between the value of services rendered and their market price? It must be remembered that market price depends upon human judgment, which is fallible, while absolute value is fixed by natural law. Have not some men been counted failures, owing to false perspective, who should be reckoned among successes? And perhaps conversely, do we not often hastily pronounce a man a success because of his accumulated profits, without counting the cost to the community?

And what is our conclusion in fine? Education, in so far as it approaches the ideal, is unquestionably conducive of the highest success, if only we have the right idea of what constitutes success: Your success is measured, not by what the world gives to you, but by what you give to the world.[4]

> *Your success is measured, not by what the world gives you, but by what you give to the world.*

Before you "find" yourself, you may require much education. You must be able to draw mental pictures of the genius you would like to be. By "education" I do not mean book learning. A child can memorize a poem and repeat it from memory perfectly yet know absolutely nothing of the meaning of the poem. Recently I met a beggar on the streets who could speak nearly a dozen languages, yet he couldn't earn a living. He was educated, in the way that we usually speak of education, but his learning was useless to him.

I also know men who can neither read nor write but have made a million dollars or more in business. They too are educated, but it is the practical sort of education.

This brings us face to face with the interesting task of finding out what an education is and how it may be obtained. I feel safe in saying that not one person in a thousand can give a correct definition of *education*. Not one in ten thousand can tell you how to get an education.

The average person who wanted to get an education would probably think first of some college or university, with the false belief that these institutions could "educate" their students. But nothing in the world would be farther from the truth. The fact of the matter is that all any school on earth can do, save one, is to prepare a foundation for acquiring an education, and that one exception is the *school of life*, through the instruction books of *human experience*. Don't forget this. Don't believe for a moment that you can buy an education for money. You can't do it. An education is something you have to work for. Furthermore, it cannot be acquired in the usual four years given over to college training. If we are good students, we are going to school always. We never get through. Life is one continuous school, and the kind of students we are depends upon the kind of work we do as we go through this great *university*.

A recent editorial in the *Chicago Examiner* gives the best description of how to acquire an education that I have ever seen. It is so good that I have reproduced it. The article is well worth the earnest consideration of anyone:

WHAT IS AN EDUCATION?

An education is an achievement, not a gift. You have to get it yourself. And the way you get it is to work for it. You have to work to get it, and then you have to work to keep it.

Education is self-discovery. It is finding out who you are, what you can understand, and what you can do. The word *education* means "to educe, to bring out, to grow, to evolve." The only way to strengthen a muscle is to use it. It is the same with the mind. The brain is an organ, and to keep it healthy you have to give it exercise. And you exercise the brain by studying, thinking, and working. Study anything half an hour a day and you will be, in a few years, a person of education.

There is no such thing as "completing your education"; it is all comparative. And in one sense the purpose of education is to teach men how little they know.

The man is best educated who is most useful.

Some of the very strongest and most influential men who have ever lived were men who had no "advantages." Of course, it is equally true that great numbers of college graduates have gone to the front, but on the other hand, a college degree is no proof of competence. And as long as some men who are not college-bred take first place on the roster of fame and other men who are college-bred sink out of sight, most thinking men are quite willing to admit that the science of education remains yet to be mastered.

Of the college men who succeed, who shall say they succeed by and through the aid the college gave, or in spite of it? Yet many men will wail—"If I only had the advantage of a college training."

If so it might have ironed all the individuality out of them.

To take a young man away from his work, say, at eighteen years of age, and keep him from useful labor in the name of education for four years, will someday be regarded as a most absurd proposition. Set in motion by philosophers, the idea was that the young man should be drilled and versed in "sacred" themes, hence the dead languages and the fixed thought that education should be an exclusive thing.

This separation from the practical world for a number of years, where no useful work was done and the whole attention fixed on abstract themes and theories, often tended to cripple the man so that he could never go back to the world of work and usefulness. He was no longer a producer and had to be supported by tithes and taxes.

In the smaller colleges many instances are found of students working their way through school. Such students stand a very much better chance in the world's race than those who are made exempt from practical affairs by having everything provided. The responsibility of caring for himself is a necessary factor in man's evolution. To make a young man exempt from the practical world from eighteen to twenty-two is to run the risk of ruining him for life. Possibly you have taken opportunity from him and turned him into a memory machine.

There are persons who are always talking about "preparation for life." The best way to prepare for life is to begin to live. A school should be life. Isolation from the world in order to prepare for the world's work is an error. You might as well take a boy out of a blacksmith shop in order to teach him blacksmithing. From the age of fourteen and upwards the pupil should feel that he is doing something useful, not merely killing time; and so his work and instruction should go right along, hand in hand.

The educated man is the useful man. And no matter how many college degrees a man has, if he cannot earn an honest living, he is not educated and is one with the yesterdays, doing pedagogic goosestep down the days to dusty death.

Within thirty years a sure evolution has been going on in the method of teaching children. The changes have been so great that they have truly amounted to a revolution. These changes in method have sprung principally from one man. That man is Friedrich Fröbel. Fröbel was the inventor and originator of the kindergarten. The kindergarten was the greatest, most important, most useful innovation of the nineteenth century.

No rapid-transit scheme of moving men from this point to that with lightning-like rapidity, no invention of calling up folks five hundred miles away and talking to them, can compare in value with that which gives love for brutality, trust for fear, hope for despair, the natural for the artificial.

The kindergarten! The "child-garden"—a place in which the little souls fresh from God bloom and blossom! You cannot make the plant blossom. You can, however, place it in the sunshine and supply it aliment and dew; but nature does the rest. So it is with teaching. All we can do is to comply with the conditions of growth in the child, and God does the rest.

> *We are strong only as we ally ourselves with nature.*

We are strong only as we ally ourselves with nature. We can make headway only by laying hold on the forces of the universe. Man is a part of nature—just as much so as are the tree and the bird. In the main, every animal and every organism does the thing that is best for it to do. Fröbel thought that human nature in all its elements is as free from falsity and error as nature is under any other aspect.

The kindergarten system is simply the utilization of play as the prime factor in education. Fröbel made the discovery that play was God's plan of educating the young, so he adopted it.

Before Fröbel's day everybody seemed to think that play was a big waste of time in the children, and a sin in the grown-ups. That which was pleasant was bad. Some folks still hold to this idea, but such folks are growing a trifle lonesome. In 1850, the year before Fröbel died, he said,

"It will take the world four hundred years to recognize the truth of my theories."

Only seventy-five years have gone, and already we find the kindergarten idea coloring the entire scheme of pedagogics. Like a single drop of aniline in a barrel of water, its influence is shown in every part.

Let us look for a day when the opportunities for education will be like the landscape: free to everyone who has the capacity to absorb. There must be no "educated class" and "superior class"—every man must feel that he is superior to taking and enjoying a thing from which others by birth and ill-fortune are barred. As long as other men are kept in prison we too are in bonds.

But the world is getting better; go and visit your public school—any school—and compare it with the school of twenty-five years ago. There is beauty on the walls, cleanliness, order, fresh air, light, and gentle consideration. Do not expect to find perfection—there is yet much work to do.

The biggest and best part of life lies in supplying yourselves the things you need, and education, which is development, comes from doing without things, making things, and talking about things you do not have, a great deal more than from using tools and instruments which rich men supply you gratis. If everything is done for us we will not do much for ourselves.

To be able to earn a living is quite as necessary as to parse a Greek verb. The reason the industrial college has never evolved is because we have not so far evolved men big enough to captain both education and industry. We have plenty of men big enough for college presidents—thousands of them—but we haven't men who can direct the energies of young men and women into useful channels and at the same time feed their expanding minds. This is where we reach our limit. There is room for the man who can set in motion a curriculum that will embrace earning a living and mental growth and have them move together hand in hand.

For the man who can weld life and education, the laurel waits. The chief error of college lies in the fact that they have separated the world of culture from the world of work. They have fostered the fallacy that one set of men should do all the hard labor and another set should have the education—that one should be ornamental and the other useful.

Education should be within the reach of every individual, not for the lucky few.

It is qualities that fit a man for life of usefulness, not the mental possession of facts. The school that best helps to form character, not the one that imparts the most information, is the college the future will demand. Is there a single college or university in the world that focuses on qualities? At many of our colleges cigarettes are optional, but a stranger seeing the devotion to them would surely suppose the practice of cigarette smoking was compulsory. The boy who does not acquire the tobacco habit at college is regarded as eccentric. The same is true, only to a less marked degree, of the liquor habit. Many of the professors teach the cigarette habit by example. At all of our great colleges, gymnasium work is optional. Instead of physical culture there is athletics, and those who need the gymnasium most are ashamed to be seen there.

I would not leave the impression that I have no use for the so-called "higher education" of which the college man feels so proud. A college education is all right for the young man or young woman who intends to take up one of the professions, provided—and here is a very dangerous point to discuss lest we make enemies—the young man or young woman does not come out of college feeling that he or she is superior to the less fortunate who haven't had a college education, and provided also that he or she does not lose his or her individuality in acquiring college training. It has required a great many years of hard experience for me to arrive at my present belief that my not having had a college education does not disqualify me from being a pretty strong competitor of those who have had one. For many years I labored under the false belief that I stood no chance of ever amounting to much or ever being able to serve the world in any very useful manner because I had not acquired a college education.

Reverses, Hard Knocks, Poverty

The best education that any man or woman ever gets is that which comes through *reverses*, *hard knocks*, and *a good taste of poverty*. What college education could compare with those experiences in life that make one thoughtful of one's fellow men? I am not saying that a college education takes away all of one's sympathy, but I do say that poverty and bitter experiences are sure sources through which to develop sympathy.

My oldest boy is now just reaching his fifth year. When he was barely able to talk so he could be easily understood, he commanded me to get the automobile and take him to the theater! From that day until this I have seen the tremendous task which I have ahead of me—the task of teaching the little fellow that the present generation is traveling in a dangerous direction and at a very dangerous speed on account of the great wealth of this country, wealth which is comparatively easy to secure. Regardless of my financial status during the next ten years, I must teach my boy that before one has a right to spend, one must earn. I confess that I dread the job.

My tendency is to "make it easy" for my boys. But, my better judgment and my actual experience tell me that the very best way to "make it easy" for them is first to "make it hard" for them! Both of my boys "turn up their noses" at a penny. Sometimes a nickel will do, but generally they demand nothing less than a quarter. I have adopted the plan of paying them regular wages. The oldest one I pay a quarter a week and the youngest one I pay ten cents a week. In return for this they must carry in the paper from the back door and help their mother by running little chores to such an extent that she will OK the payroll on Saturday night before they get their pay. Any disobedience may cost a fine of a nickel. Some of the more serious disobediences may cost an entire week's wages.

These are simple matters of a family routine, but as my boys grow older I shall continue to lay a practical foundation for an education that shall enable them to *make a good living and be of service to the world.* This would be impossible unless I taught them the value of good, wholesome work.

I do not wish to be poor. None of us who have gone through this experience ever care to go through it again. Those of us who are still laboring under its painful lash want to get out of its clutches just as rapidly as we can. But, I do want my boys to know the value of poverty, just as I know it. *I want them to have this necessary foundation for an education.* Then, whether they go through college or not, if they learn the lesson of poverty properly they will be able to compete with the more fortunate ones who have had a college training.

The majority of the people of the world have not had a college education. My message on the subject of *the man who has had no chance* is intended to lend hope and encouragement to this large class of worthy people. If you are one of that number, let me assure you that a good stock of self-confidence backed by plenty of hope and good cheer is more than the equivalent of a college degree. Without this very necessary stock of human qualities, no college degree on earth would be worth to you the parchment on which it was written.

If I were called upon to drink health to a man whom I considered the greatest success, I would drink to *the man who has had no chance.* It will be upon his shoulders that the destiny of the world will depend. Already he is carrying the burdens of the world, both commercially and socially. He is managing our railroads, or banks, our great industrial corporations. Nay, he is directing the affairs of the greatest nations of the world. Hats off to *the man who has had no chance.* We all owe him homage. Yet he is the plainest man among us. He is the least exciting, the most sympathetic and kind. He enjoys with us our successes and suffers with us our troubles.

Do not pity him—envy him! If you belong to his class then enjoy the greatest heritage that can come to a human being.

In 1922, Napoleon Hill was invited to give the commencement address at Salem College in Salem, West Virginia. The school was founded in 1888 as a liberal arts, teacher education, and nursing college. Titled "The End of the Rainbow," the commencement address was the most influential speech that Hill ever gave.

When Hill delivered the speech in 1922, he was thirty-nine years old and had many years' experience in writing and speaking, but he was still several years away from publishing his first book. He was passionately focused on his speechmaking and lectured anywhere he could get an audience. As Hill became better known, especially after he became a published author, his lectures were in great demand. In the archives of the Napoleon Hill Foundation are recorded the data of eighty-nine speeches he gave throughout the country—all in just one year.

The 1922 speech Hill gave at Salem College inspired a letter he received years later from a member of Congress, Jennings Randolph. Hill was to mention this letter (available to read in the appendix of this book) in the introduction to his 1937 book *Think and*

Grow Rich, and to print Randolph's inspirational letter. Randolph won his seat in Congress in 1932, the same year that Franklin D. Roosevelt was elected president of the United States.

Randolph introduced Hill to Roosevelt, and Hill became an unpaid advisor to the president during the Great Depression. Written correspondence from the White House is contained in the Napoleon Hill Foundation's archives.

Randolph would later become a US Senator and a trustee of the Napoleon Hill Foundation. He died in 1998 and was the last member of Congress to have served in the beginning of the Franklin D. Roosevelt Administration.

The recovery of the newspaper account of the speech is the result of the diligent work of Dr. J. B. Hill, grandson of Napoleon Hill, who was able to obtain the speech from microfilm, and Dr. J. B. Hill's wife, Nancy, who retyped it. The following is that speech.

—DON GREEN

The End of the Rainbow

1922 Commencement Address at Salem College

by
Napoleon Hill

There is a legend as old as the human race that tells us that a pot of gold can be found at the end of a rainbow. This fairy tale, which grips the imaginative child's mind, may have something to do with the present tendency of the human race to look for the easy way to find riches. For nearly twenty years I sought the end of my rainbow that I might claim that pot of gold. My struggle in search of the evasive rainbow's end was ceaseless. It carried me up the mountainside of failure and down the hillsides of despair, luring me on and on in search of the phantom pot of gold.

I was sitting before a fire one night discussing with older people the question of unrest upon the part of laboring men.

The labor union movement had just begun to make itself felt in that part of the country where I then lived, and the tactics used by the labor organizers impressed me as being too revolutionary and obstructive ever to bring permanent success. One of the men who sat before that fireside with me made a comment that proved to be one of the best pieces of advice that I have ever followed. He reached over and firmly grasped me by the shoulders, looked me squarely in the eyes, and said: "Why, you are a bright boy, and if you will give yourself an education, you will make your mark in this world."[5]

The first concrete result of that remark caused me to enroll in a local business college, a step which I am duty-bound to admit proved to be one of the most helpful that I ever took because I got my first fleeting glimpse in business college of what one might call a *fair sense of proportions.*[6] After completing business college, I obtained a position as a stenographer and bookkeeper and worked in this capacity for several years.[7]

As a result of this idea of *performing more service and better service than paid for,* which I had learned in business college, I advanced rapidly and always succeeded in filling positions of responsibility far in advance of my years, with salary proportionate.

I saved money and soon had a bank account amounting to several thousand dollars. I was rapidly advancing toward my rainbow's end.

My reputation spread rapidly and I found competitive bidders for my services. I was in demand, not because of what I knew, which was little enough, but because of *my willingness to make the best use of what little I did know.* This spirit of willingness proved to be the most powerful and strategic principle I ever learned.[8]

The tides of fate blew me southward and I became sales manager for a large lumber manufacturing concern. I knew nothing about lumber and I knew nothing about sales management, but I had learned that it was *well to render better service and more of it than I was paid for;* and with this principle as the dominant spirit, I tackled my job with the determination to find out all I could about selling lumber.

I made a good record. My salary was increased twice during the year and my bank account was growing bigger and bigger. I did so well in managing the sales of my employer's lumber that he organized a new lumber company and took me into partnership with him.

I could see myself growing nearer and nearer to the rainbow's end. Money and success poured in to me from every direction, all of which fixed my attention steadfastly on the pot of gold that I could plainly see just ahead of me. Up to this time it did not occur to me that success could consist of anything except gold!

The Unseen Hand

The "Unseen Hand" allowed me to strut around under the influence of my vanity until I had begun to feel my importance. In the light of more sober years and a more accurate interpretation of human events I now wonder if the "Unseen Hand" does not purposely permit us foolish human beings to parade before our own mirror of vanity until we see how vulgar we are and stop it.

At any rate, I seemed to have a clear track ahead; there was coal in the bunker, water in the tank, my hand was on the throttle and I opened it wide. Fate was awaiting me just around the bend with a stuffed club, and it wasn't stuffed with cotton. And I did not see the impending crash until it came.

Like a stroke of lightning out of the clear blue sky, an economic collapse and panic crashed down on me. Overnight it swept away every dollar that I had. The man with whom I was in business withdrew, panic-stricken but without loss, and left me with nothing but the empty shell of a company that owned nothing except a good reputation. I could have bought a hundred thousand dollars of lumber on that reputation.

A crooked lawyer saw a chance to cash in on that reputation and what was left of the lumber company on my hands. He and a group of other men purchased the company and continued to operate it. I learned later that they bought every dollar worth of lumber that they could get, resold it, and pocketed the proceeds without paying for it. Thus, I had been the innocent means of helping them defraud their creditors, who learned when it was too late that I was in no way connected with the company.

It required an economic collapse and the next failure that it brought to me to divert and redirect my efforts from the lumber business to the study of law. Nothing on earth but failure, or what I then called failure, could have brought about that result. Thus, a turning point of my life was ushered in on the wings of failure. *There is a great lesson in every failure whether we know what it is or not.*[9]

When I entered law school, it was with the firm belief that I would emerge doubly prepared to catch up with the end of the rainbow and claim my pot of gold. I still had no higher aspiration than that of accumulating money; yet, the very thing that I worshiped most seemed to be the most elusive thing on earth, for it was always evading me, always in sight, but always just out of reach.

I attended law school at night and worked as an automobile salesman during the day. My sales experience in the lumber business was turned to good advantage. I prospered rapidly, doing so well from *the habit of performing more and better service than paid for* that the opportunity came to open a school to train ordinary machinists in automotive assembly and repair work. This school prospered until it was paying me a large monthly salary. Again I had my rainbow's end in sight. Again I knew that I had at last found my niche in the world's work. Again I knew that nothing could swerve me from my course or cause me to divert my attention.

My banker saw me prospering. He extended me credit for expansion. He encouraged me to invest in outside lines of business. He appeared to me to be one of the finest men in the world. He loaned me many thousands of dollars on my signature, without endorsement.

My banker loaned me money until I was hopelessly in his debt and then he took over my business. It all happened so suddenly that it dazed me. I didn't think such a thing possible. You see, I still had much to learn about the ways of men, especially the kind of man that unfortunately my banker turned out to be—a type which, in justice to the business of banking, I ought to say is rare.

> *This failure was one of the greatest blessings that ever was bestowed upon me.*

From a man of affairs earning a good income, owner of half a dozen automobiles and much other junk which I didn't need, I was reduced to poverty. The rainbow's end disappeared, and it was many years before I learned that *this failure was one of the greatest blessings that ever was bestowed upon me* because it forced me out of a business which in no way helped me develop the human side and diverted my efforts into a channel that brought me an experience that I greatly needed.

I think it is worthy of note to state here that I went back to Washington, DC, a few years after the event and out of curiosity visited the old bank where I once had a liberal line of credit, expecting, of course, to find it still in operation. To my great surprise I found that the bank had gone out of business, and my erstwhile banker had been reduced to penury and want. I met him on the street, practically penniless. With eyes red and swollen, he aroused in me a questioning attitude, and I wondered for the first time in my life if one might find any other thing of value except money at the rainbow's end.

Because I was my wife's husband and her people had influence, I secured an appointment as assistant to the chief counsel for a family-owned business. My salary was greatly out of proportion to the wages that the company usually paid beginners, and still further out of proportion to what I was worth; but pull is pull, and I was there because I was there.

It turned out that what I lacked in legal ability, I supplied through that one sound, fundamental principle that I had learned in business college—namely, *to render more service and better service than paid for*, whenever possible.

I was holding my position without any difficulty. I practically had a berth for life if I cared to keep it. One day, I did what my close personal friends and relatives said was a very foolish thing: I quit my job abruptly.

When pressed for a reason, I gave what seemed to me to be a very sound one, but I had trouble convincing the family circle that I had acted wisely, and still greater difficulty convincing a few of my friends that I was perfectly rational in mind. I quit that job because I found the work too easy and demanding too little effort and I found myself drifting.[10]

This move proved to be an important turning point in my life, although it was followed by ten years of effort that brought almost every grief that the human heart could experience. I quit my job in the legal field, where I was getting along well, living among friends and relatives with what they believed to be a bright and unusually promising future, and I moved to Chicago.

I selected Chicago because I believed it to be the most competitive place in the world. I felt that if I could go to Chicago and gain recognition along any legitimate line, I would prove to myself that I had the material in me that might, some day, develop into real ability.

In Chicago, I secured the position of advertising manager.[11] I knew next to nothing about advertising, but my previous experience as a salesman came to my rescue, and my old friend, *the habit of performing more services than paid for*, gave me a fair balance on the credit side of the ledger.

The first year I flourished. I was coming back by leaps and bounds. Gradually, the rainbow began to circle around me, and I saw once more that shining pot of gold almost within reach. I believe it of importance to recall the fact that my standard of success was always measured in terms of dollars and my rainbow's end promised nothing but a pot of gold. Up to this point, if the thought that anything except gold might be found at the end of the rainbow, that thought was momentary and quickly vanished. History is full of evidence that a feast usually precedes a fall. I was having my feast but never thought of the fall. I suspect that no one ever anticipates the fall until it comes, but come it will, unless one's fundamental guiding principles are sound.

I made a good record as an advertising manager. The president of the company was attracted by my work and later helped organize the Betsy Ross Candy Company, and I became its president, thus beginning the next most important turning point of my life and the prelude to another failure.[12]

The business began to expand until we had a chain of stores in many different cities.[13] Again I saw my rainbow's end almost within reach. I knew that I had at last found the business in which I wanted to remain for life, and I frankly admit that our business was fashioned after that of another candy company whose western manager was my personal friend. His overwhelming success was the main factor in causing me to enter the candy business.

Everything went smoothly for a time, until my business associate and a third man whom we later took into the business conceived the notion to gain control of my interests without paying for it, a mistake that men never seem to understand that they are making until it is too late and they have paid the price of their folly.

The Plan Worked

The plan worked, but I balked more stiffly than they had anticipated; therefore, to gently urge me along toward the grand exit, they had me arrested on a false charge and offered to settle out of court if I would turn over my interest in the company.

I refused and insisted on going to trial. When the time arrived for court, no one was present to prosecute. We insisted on prosecution and requested the court to summon the complaining witness and make him prosecute, which was done.

The judge, the Honorable Arnold Heap, stopped the proceedings and threw the case out of court before it had gone very far, with the statement that "this is one of the most flagrant cases of attempted coercion that has ever come before me."

To protect my reputation I brought suit for fifty thousand dollars in damages. The case was tried five years later and I secured a heavy judgment in the Superior Court of Chicago. The suit was a "tort action," meaning that it claimed damages for the libelous injury to my reputation.

But I suspect that another and much more exacting law than that under which tort actions may be brought was operating during those five years because one of the parties—the one who originated the scheme to have me arrested as part of the plan to force my interests in the business away from me—was serving a term in the federal penitentiary before my action against him was tried, and for a crime separate and apart from the one he had committed against me. The other party had fallen from a high station in life to poverty and disgrace.

My judgment stands in the records of the Superior Court of Chicago as silent evidence of the vindication of my character and as evidence of something far more important than mere vindication; namely, that the "Unseen Hand" which guides the destiny of all who earnestly seek truth had eliminated from my nature all desire for my pound of flesh. My judgment against my transducers was not collected, and it never will be!

At least, I will never collect it, because I suspect that it has been paid many times over in blood and remorse and regret and failure visited upon those who would have destroyed my character for personal gain.

This was one of the greatest single blessings that ever came to me because it taught me to forgive! It taught me also that the *law of compensation is always in operation and that "Whatsoever a man soweth, that shall he also reap."*[14] It blotted out of my nature the last lingering thought of seeking personal revenge at any time under any circumstances. It taught me that time is the friend of all who are right and the mortal enemy of all who are unjust and destructive in their efforts. It brought me nearer to a full understanding of the Master when he said, "Forgive them Father for they know not what they do."

Teaching

We now come to another venture that probably brought me nearer the rainbow's end than any of the others because it placed me in a position where I found it necessary to bring all the knowledge that I had acquired up to that time, concerning every subject with which I was familiar, and gave me opportunity for self-expression and personal development such as rarely comes to a man so early in life.

I turned my efforts toward teaching advertising and salesmanship.[15]

Some wise philosopher has said that we never learn much until we start trying to teach others. My experience as a teacher proved that this is true. My school prospered from the start. I had a resident school and a correspondent school through which I was teaching students in nearly every English-speaking country.

In spite of the ravages of war, my school was growing by leaps and bounds, and I saw the end of my rainbow drawing nearer and nearer. I was so close that I could almost reach out and touch the pot of gold.

As a result of the record that I was making and the recognition I was gaining, I attracted the attention of the head of a corporation, who employed me for three weeks out of each month at a salary of $105,200 a year—considerably more than the president of the United States receives.

In less than six months, I built up one of the most efficient working forces in America and increased the assets of the company to a point where it was offered twenty million dollars more for its business than it was worth when I started.

Candidly, had you been in my place, would you not have felt justified in saying that you found your rainbow's end? Would you have felt justified in saying that you had attained success?

I thought I had, but I had one of the rudest shocks of all awaiting me, due partly to the dishonesty of the head of the corporation for whom I was working, but more directly, I suspect, to a deeper and more significant cause concerning which fate seemed to have decreed that I should learn something.

One hundred thousand dollars of my salary was conditional upon my remaining as the directing head of staff for a period of one year. In less than half that time, I began to see that I was pyramiding power and placing it in the hands of a man who was growing power-drunk. I began to see that ruin awaited him just around the corner. This discovery brought me much grief.

Morally, I was responsible for several million dollars of capital that I had induced the American people to invest in this corporation. Legally, of course, I was in no way responsible.

I finally brought this matter to a head, delivering an ultimatum to the head of the corporation to safeguard the funds of the company under a board of financial control or else accept my resignation. He laughed at the suggestion because he thought I would not break my contract and thereby lose one hundred thousand dollars. Perhaps I would not have done so had it not been for the moral responsibility that I felt on behalf of the thousands of investors. I resigned and the company passed into the hands of receivership, and therefore I did all I could to protect it against the mismanagement of a money-mad young man, a bit of satisfaction that brought me much ridicule and cost me one hundred thousand dollars.

For the moment my rainbow's end seemed vague and somewhat distant. There were moments when I wondered what caused me to make a fool of myself and throw away a fortune just to protect those who never would even know that I had made sacrifices for them.

In my climax, I will tabulate the sum total of all that I have learned from each of the important failures and mileposts of my life, but first let me describe the last of those failures. To do so, I must go back to that eventful day— November 11, 1918. That was Armistice Day, as everyone knows. Like most other people, I became as drunk with enthusiasm and joy as any man ever did on wine.

I was practically penniless, as the war had destroyed my business, and I had turned my efforts to war work; but I was happy to know that the slaughter was over and reason was about to spread its beneficial wings over the earth once more. The war had swept away my school, from which my income would have amounted to over fifteen thousand dollars a year had our students not been drafted for war and had I not felt it my own duty to turn my efforts to helping my country in its time of need. I stood as far away from my rainbow's end as I did on that eventful day more than twenty years previously when I looked into the drift mouth of a coal mine where I was employed as a laborer, and thought of that statement that a kindly old gentleman had made to me the night before, but realized that a yawning chasm stood between me and any accomplishment other than a laborer in the mines.

Happy Again

But I was happy again! Again that tramp thought entered my consciousness and prompted me to ask myself if I had not been searching for the wrong sort of reward at my rainbow's end. I sat down to my typewriter with nothing particular in mind. To my astonishment, my hands began to play a regular symphony upon the keys of the typewriter. I had never written so rapidly or easily before. I did not think of what I was writing—I just wrote and wrote and kept on writing.

When I was through, I had five pages of manuscript, and as near as I have been able to determine, that manuscript was written without any organized thoughts on my part. It was an editorial out of which my first magazine, *Napoleon Hill's Golden Rule Magazine,* was born. I took this editorial to a wealthy man and read it to him. Before I had read the last line, he had promised to finance my magazine. It was in this somewhat dramatic manner that a desire that had lain dormant in my mind for nearly twenty years began to express itself. It was the same idea that I had in mind when I made the statement that caused that old gentleman to lay his hand on my shoulder and make that fortunate remark twenty years previously, which had at its foundation the thought that the Golden Rule ought to be the guiding spirit in all human relationships.

All my life I had wanted to become a newspaper editor. More than twenty years ago, when I was a very small boy, I used to kick the press for my father, who published a small newspaper, and I grew to love the smell of printer's ink.

The important thing to which I would direct your attention is the fact that I found my proper niche in the world's work and I was very happy in it. Strangely enough, I entered upon this work, which constituted my last lap in the long, long trail over which I had traveled in search of my rainbow's end, with never a thought of finding a pot of gold.

The magazine prospered from the beginning. In less than six months, it was being read in every English-speaking country in the world. It has brought me recognition from all parts of the world, which resulted in a public speaking tour in 1920 covering every large city in America.

Up to now, I had made about as many enemies as I had friends. Now a strange thing has happened: beginning with my initial editorial work, I commenced to make friends by the thousands until today upwards of one hundred thousand people stand squarely back of me because they believe in me and my message.

What brought about this change?

If you understand the law of attraction, you can answer this because you know that like attracts like and that a man will attract friends or foes according to the nature of the thoughts that dominate his mind. One cannot take a belligerent attitude toward life and expect to make friends. When I commenced to preach the Golden Rule in my first magazine, I started to live it as near as I could.

There is a big difference between merely believing in the Golden Rule and actually practicing it in overt acts, a truth I learned when I began my first magazine. This realization brought me abruptly into an understanding of a principle that now permeates every thought that finds a permanent lodging place in my mind and dominates every act I perform as nearly as humanly possible, and that thought is none other than the one laid down by the Master in his Sermon on the Mount when he admonished us to "do unto others as we would have others do unto us."

During these past three years since, I have been sending out Golden Rule thought vibrations to hundreds of thousands of people. These thought waves have multiplied themselves in the rebound and have brought back to me floods of goodwill from those whom my message reached.

I was rapidly approaching my rainbow's end for the seventh and last time. Every avenue of failure seemed closed. My enemies had been slowly transformed into friends and I was making new friends by the thousands. But there was a final test to undergo.

As I have stated, I was approaching the end of my rainbow with the firm belief that nothing on earth could stop me from attaining it and obtaining my pot of gold and everything else that a successful searcher for that great reward might expect.

Like a stroke of lightning out of the clear sky, I received a shock!

The impossible had happened. My first magazine, *Napoleon Hill's Golden Rule Magazine*, was not only snatched out of my hand overnight, but its influence that I had built up was temporarily turned as a weapon against me.

Again, man had failed me, and I thought unkind thoughts about man. It was a savage blow to me when I awoke to the realization that there was no truth to the Golden Rule that I had been preaching to thousands of people through the pages of my magazine and in person and had been doing my level best to live as well.

This was the supreme moment of testing.

Had my experience proved my most beloved principle to be false and nothing more than a snare with which to trip the untutored, or was I about to learn a great lesson which would establish the truth and soundness of those principles for the remainder of my life and perhaps throughout eternity?

These were the questions that pressed upon me.

I did not answer them quickly; I could not. I was so stunned that I had to stop and catch my breath. I had been preaching that one could not steal another man's ideas, or plans, or goods and wares and still prosper. My experience seemed to give the lie to all I had ever written or spoken along this line because the men who stole the child of my heart and brain seemed not only to be prospering with it, but they had actually used it as a means of stopping me from carrying out my plans for worldwide service in the interest of the human race.

Months passed by, and I was unable to turn a wheel.

I had been deposed, my magazine had been taken away from me, and my friends seemed to look upon me as a sort of fallen Richard the Lionheart. Some said I would come back stronger and bigger for the experience. Others said I was through. Thus the remarks came and went, but I stood looking on in wonderment, feeling much the same as a person feels who is undergoing a nightmare and so cannot awaken or move as much as a finger.

Literally I was experiencing a wide-awake nightmare that seemed to hold me firmly within its grasp. My courage was gone. My faith in humanity was all but gone. My love for humanity was weakening. Slowly but surely I was reversing my opinion concerning the highest and best ideals that I had been building for more than a score of years. The passing weeks seemed like an eternity. The days seemed like a whole lifetime.

One day the atmosphere began to clear.

Some cloudy atmospheres usually do clear away. Time is a wonderful healer of wounds. Time cures nearly everything that is sick or ignorant, and most of us are both at times.

> *Time cures nearly everything*
> *that is sick or ignorant, and*
> *most of us are both at times.*

During the seventh and greatest failure of my life, I was reduced to greater poverty than any I had ever known before. From a well-furnished home, I was reduced practically overnight to a one-room apartment. Coming as this blow did, just as I was about to lay hold of the pot of gold at my rainbow's end, it cut a deep and ugly wound in my heart. During this brief testing spell, I was made to kneel in the very dust of poverty and eat the crust of all my past follies. When I had all but given up, the clouds of darkness began to float away as rapidly as they had come.

I stood face to face with one of the most trying tests that ever came to me. Perhaps no human being ever was more severely tried than I was—at least that was the way I felt about it at the time.

The postman had delivered my scant collection of mail. As I opened it, I was watching the pale red sun as it had all but disappeared over the western horizon. To me it was symbolic of that which was about to happen to me, for I saw my sun of hope also setting in the west. I opened the envelope on top, and as I did so, a certificate of deposit fluttered to the floor and fell face upward. It was for twenty-five thousand dollars. For a whole minute I stood with my eyes glued to that bit of paper, wondering if I were not dreaming. I walked over closer to it, picked it up, and read the letter accompanying it.

That money was mine! I could draw it out of the bank at will. Only two slight strings were attached to it, but these strings made it necessary to obligate myself morally to turn my back on everything that I had been preaching about, placing the interest of the people above those of any individual.

The supreme moment of testing had come. Would I accept that money which was ample capital with which to publish my magazine or would I return it and carry on a little longer? These were the first questions that claimed my attention.

Then I heard the ringing of a bell in the region of my heart. This time its sound was more direct. It caused the blood to tingle through my body. With the ringing of the bell came the most direct command that ever registered itself in my consciousness, and that command was accompanied by a chemical change in my brain such as I had never experienced before. It was a positive, startling command, and it brought a message that I could not misunderstand.

Without promise of a reward, it made me return that twenty-five thousand dollars.

I hesitated. That bell kept on ringing. My feet seemed glued to the spot. I could not move out of my tracks. Then I reached my decision. I decided to heed that prompting, which no one but a fool could have mistaken.

The instant I reached this conclusion, I looked, and in the approaching twilight, I saw the rainbow's end. I had at last caught up with it. I saw no pot of gold except the one I was about to send back to the source from which it came, but I found something more precious than all the gold in the world, as I heard a voice that reached me, not through my ears, but through my heart.

And it said: "Standeth God within the shadow of every failure."

The end of my rainbow brought me the triumph of principle over gold. It gave me a closer communion with the great "Unseen Force" of this universe and new determination to plant the seed of the Golden Rule philosophically in the hearts of millions of other weary travelers who are seeking the end of their rainbow.

> **The end of my rainbow brought me the triumph of principle over gold.**

In the July 1921 issue of *Napoleon Hill's Magazine*, my secretary tells of one of the most dramatic events that followed closely upon my decision not to accept financial help from sources that would in any extent whatsoever control my pen. That incident is only one, each constituting sufficient evidence to convince all but fools that the Golden Rule really works, that the law of compensation is in operation, and that "Whatsoever a man soweth, that shall he also reap."

Not alone did I get all the capital necessary to carry *Napoleon Hill's Magazine* over the beginning period, during which its own revenues were insufficient to publish it, but what is of greater significance—the magazine is growing with rapidity heretofore unknown in the field of similar periodicals. The readers and the public generally have caught the spirit of the work we are doing and they have put the law of increasing returns into operation in our favor.

The Most Important Lessons

Now let me summarize the most important lessons I learned in my search for the rainbow's end. I will not try to mention all the lessons but only the most important ones. I will leave to your own imagination much that you can see without my recounting it here.

First and most important of all, in my search for the rainbow's end, I found God in every concrete, understandable, and satisfying manifestation, which is quite significant if I found nothing more. All my life I had been somewhat unsettled as to the exact nature of that "Unseen Hand" which directs the affairs of the universe, but my seven turning points on the rainbow trail of life brought me, at last, to a conclusion that satisfies. Whether my conclusion is right or wrong is not of much importance; the main thing is that it satisfies me.

The lessons of importance that I learned are these:

I learned that those whom we consider our enemies are in reality our friends. In the light of all that has happened, I would not begin to go back and undo a single one of these trying experiences with which I met because each one of them brought to me positive evidence of the soundness of the Golden Rule and the existence of the law of compensation, through which we claim our rewards for virtue and pay the penalties for our ignorance.

I learned that time is a friend of all who base their thoughts and actions on truth and justice and that it is the mortal enemy of all who fail to do so, even though the penalty of the reward is often slow in arriving where it is due.

I learned that the only pot of gold worth striving for is that which comes from the satisfaction of knowing that one's efforts are bringing happiness to others.

One by one I have seen those who are unjust with me cut down by failure. I have lived to see every one of them reduced to failure far beyond anything that they planned against me. The banker whom I mentioned was reduced to poverty; the men who stole my interest in the Betsy Ross Candy Company and tried to destroy my reputation have come down to what looks like permanent failure, one of them living as a convict in a federal prison.

The man who defrauded me out of my one hundred thousand-dollar salary and whom I elevated to wealth and influence has been reduced to poverty and want. At every turn of the road that led finally to my rainbow's end I saw undisputable evidence to back the Golden Rule philosophy that I am now sending forth through organized effort to hundreds of thousands of people.

Lastly, I have learned to listen for the ringing of the bell that guides me when I come to the crossroads of doubt and hesitancy. I have learned to tap a heretofore unknown source from which I get my promptings when I wish to know which way to turn and what to do, and these promptings have never led me in the wrong direction. As I finish, I see on the walls of my study the portraits of great men whose lives I have tried to emulate. Among them is that immortal Lincoln, from whose rugged, careworn face I seem to see a smile emerging and from whose lips I can all but hear the magic words: "With charity to all and malice toward none." And deep down in my heart, I hear that mysterious bell ringing, and bellowing it comes once more as I close these lines with the greatest message that ever reached my consciousness: "Standeth God within the shadow of every failure."

When Napoleon Hill was asked to deliver the baccalaureate sermon on June 2, 1957, at Salem College, it had been thirty-five years since he had delivered a commencement address to the 1922 graduating class at the same college.

In *The Alumni Echoes,* the school paper of Salem College, the headline read "Convocation Set Today." The paper had the following to say about Dr. Hill:

> Napoleon Hill, philosopher, author, and educator who has taught more people how to achieve financial and spiritual success in life than any other living person, will deliver the baccalaureate address at 8:00 p.m. on Sunday, June 2, in the Salem College auditorium.
>
> During a personally exciting life, he developed the "science of success," an exact study which laid down the principles by which anyone can realize his material goals no matter what ambitions they may be.
>
> Mr. Hill has, moreover, been the confidant and adviser to presidents, industrialists, and government leaders including Franklin D.

Roosevelt, Woodrow Wilson, Andrew Carnegie, and Henry Ford. In fact, it was Carnegie who first started him on the research that resulted in Mr. Hill's development of the "seventeen principles of success."

Literally millions of persons credit Mr. Hill with inspiring them to greater heights of fortune in life than they ever believed possible. More than that, he has furnished them with practical step-by-step methods for realizing their ambitions.

"What the human mind can conceive and believe, the human mind can achieve" is the core of Mr. Hill's philosophy.

"You can," he says, "be anything you want to be, if only you believe with sufficient conviction—and act in accordance with your faith."

It is estimated that sixty million people throughout the world have read and benefited from his most notable book, *Think and Grow Rich*, since it was published in 1937.

Napoleon Hill was born in Wise County, Virginia, on October 26, 1883, amidst "moonshiners, mountain stills, illiteracy, and deadly feuds." Although born in poverty, it was said he was given the unusual name of Napoleon in honor of his rich paternal great uncle.

With a view toward financing his further education, Mr. Hill launched a new project at the age of twenty-five. He began writing biographical articles about successful people for Senator Bob Taylor of Tennessee, publisher of an important periodical of the day.

Rep. Jennings Randolph, who credited Hill with helping him to achieve his own success as an executive of Capital Airlines, introduced Mr. Hill in 1933 to Franklin D. Roosevelt, and as a result, Hill became a presidential advisor. It was he who gave FDR the idea for his famous speech—*"We have nothing to fear but fear itself"*—which helped halt financial hysteria at the pit of the Depression.

Mr. Hill was interested in and helpful to Salem College long years ago and delivered the commencement address in 1922. He is the publisher of *Success Unlimited* magazine. He is also the author of many books on personal improvement, including *Think and Grow Rich,* which has sold more than sixty million copies and has been reprinted in the languages of other countries. One of his more recent volumes was *How to Raise Your Own Salary.*

Hill is married and has three adult sons. He and his wife live quietly in Glendale, California.

Much had happened in the life of Hill since 1922 when he addressed the twenty-five graduates including Jennings Randolph, who was to represent West Virginia in Congress. Mr. Randolph served for many years in the US Congress and became a friend to Hill and later served as trustee in the board of the Napoleon Hill Foundation.

At the 1957 address, Hill was awarded an honorary doctorate in literature.

—DON GREEN

The Five Essentials of Success

1957 Baccalaureate Sermon at Salem College

by
Napoleon Hill

The dictionary describes a baccalaureate as—and here I quote—"a farewell sermon to a graduating class at commencement."

What I have to say to you does not constitute a sermon, and it certainly isn't a farewell!

Actually, my message to you is one of greeting, for it's my great pleasure and honor to extend a hearty welcome as you leave the scholastic world and enter the business and professional world.

I sincerely hope that my oratorical powers are sufficient to make my message highly personal so that each of you young ladies and gentlemen feel that I am speaking directly to you. For it is on this personal note that I think you will derive the greatest benefit from what I have to say.

In other words, I hope that when I've finished, you won't feel like the woman who shook hands with her minister after church one Sunday and said: "That was a wonderful sermon! Everything said applies to somebody or other I know!"

Or I might cite the case of the clergyman who illustrated a point in his sermon by saying something about which of us grows best in sunlight and which of us must have shade.

"You know," the minister told his congregation, "that you plant roses in the sunlight. But if you want fuchsias to grow, they must be kept in a shady nook."

Afterwards, the minister's heart glowed when a woman grasped his hand and said: "Pastor, I'm so grateful for your splendid sermon!" But his gratification subsided when she went on to say: "You know, I never knew before just what was the matter with my fuchsias!"

> *I hope that each of you will learn how to plant certain seeds that will reap you a rich harvest of spiritual and material happiness.*

I'm afraid that none of you will learn how to grow fuchsias from me today. But in a sense, my message *does* apply to gardening. For from my words I hope that each of you will learn how to plant certain seeds that, in years to come, will reap you a rich harvest of spiritual and material happiness.

And if each of you learns just one little tip on how to cultivate the garden of life—like the lady with her fuchsias—I shall be satisfied.

On the other hand, I hope you won't go away feeling like the little girl who attended church for the first time. When the minister asked her how she liked the service, she replied: "Well, I thought the music was very nice—but your commercial was too long!" Just thirty-five years ago this summer I stood on this same rostrum and addressed the graduating class of Salem College.

That was in 1922. World War I had just ended. In that great conflict America had been the deciding factor in bringing victory to the Allies. Our country was just emerging as the greatest political and economic power on earth. Consequently, it took no great power of prophecy for me to draw a beautiful picture for the Salem College graduating class of 1922. I was able, at that time, to call the attention of the graduates to the abundance of opportunities for personal advancement in this nation. And I was able to predict accurately that our country was entering upon its greatest period of industrial and economic expansion in history. There were some things that—I'm glad to say—I could not foresee. One of these was the Great Depression of the thirties.

The other was World War II and the rise of Communism. It almost seems as though blessed Providence lifts the veil of the future a bit to let us forecast the good things ahead of us but mercifully withholds knowledge of forthcoming evil! It has been a great pleasure to me during these past thirty-five years to watch unfold many of the predictions I made on that summer's day in 1922. I must admit, however, that my wildest, most optimistic dreams on that day came nowhere near to depicting the glorious reality! No doubt there are in today's audience at least a few from the graduating class of 1922. And I'm certain that they will forgive me for failing then to foresee the stupendous advances that man would make in the fields of science and culture. For who—in 1922—could have predicted such things as nuclear energy, the tremendous growth of the aviation and electronics industries, or our conquest of distance and time? Why, if I had dared to predict in 1922 that man would fly two and three times the speed of sound, I feel certain that members of the faculty and the graduating class would have laughed me off the stage.

(Looking at the college president) Isn't that so?

There is a great lesson for you young people in all this. It's simply this: no matter how optimistic and hopeful my words sound today, no matter how I let my imagination roam, no matter how glowingly I describe the future, I cannot possibly hope to draw a full picture of the glorious achievements mankind will accomplish during the next thirty-five years!

At this point I'm reminded of the taxicab driver in Washington, DC, who drove a tourist past the Government Archives Building. On the building there is carved a motto that reads:

"What is Past is Prologue."

"What does the motto mean?" the visitor asked.

"Well," said the driver, "it means you ain't seen nothing yet!"

The things you are destined to see during your lifetime, the glorious accomplishments in which you will take part, defy description!

Many years ago, I propounded a theory that has since been repeated so often that it now sounds like a platitude. The fact remains, however, that the truth of my statement is being proved every day. What was that statement? Simply this:

Whatever the mind of man can conceive and believe, the mind can achieve!

Truly, my young friends, your future—your attainments and achievements—will be limited only by the limits of your imagination!

There is no doubt that each of you will experience disappointments and temporary setbacks. And there's no doubt either that collective tragedy—possibly in the form of war or depression—will afflict your generation as it did those that went before you.

But here I can offer you another truth from the science of personal achievement that was my pleasure to formulate during the past fifty years: that is, that every adversity carries with it the seed of an equivalent benefit. Let me repeat that: *Every adversity carries with it the seed of an equivalent benefit.*

It's Up to You

It's up to you, however, to find this seed, nurture it, and bring it to full growth and fruition. No one can do this for you. Each of us, with the help of our Almighty Creator, creates our own destiny. And by like token, each of us must find those hidden benefits that he grants us in moments of adversity.

Let me repeat once more those two statements that I think form the pillars upon which you may, with faith, build the structure of a successful life. The first is, *whatever the mind of man can conceive and believe, the mind can achieve.* Secondly, *every adversity carries with it the seed of an equivalent benefit.*

If you master these two concepts, you will have taken two giant strides toward achieving happiness.

You have already set yourself on the road to success through the effort and work and perseverance you've demonstrated during the past four years. During this period, you have—with the splendid help of the Salem College faculty—prepared the soil of life's garden, cultivating and feeding it in preparation for planting.

Don't let anyone try to minimize the value of your college education. It has given you a tremendous advantage for shaping your future. Only as the years roll by will you come to the full realization of the help you have received from the fine men and women of the college staff. And with every passing year I'm sure you'll find reason for ever-greater gratitude toward them.

Now, with your graduation from Salem you are about to start planting the actual seeds from which you will reap a harvest later in life. There is one warning I would like to give you in this regard: Don't wait too long to start planting! Now, in the springtime of your life, is the time to decide exactly what sort of a harvest you want your life to yield. The longer you delay planting, the longer the harvest is delayed.

And this, my friends, brings me to the heart of my talk with you today.

I have been asked to tell you what I consider to be the five essential characteristics or traits that lead to success in life.

Why, you may ask, am I qualified to speak on this subject of success? I hope throughout your lifetime you will always keep the same questioning attitude regarding anyone who claims to speak with authority.

Well, Oliver Goldsmith once said that "you can preach a better sermon with your life than with your lips." So perhaps you'll indulge me for a moment if I state my qualifications to speak on the subject of personal achievement.

It was in 1908 that, as a young magazine writer, I came into contact with Andrew Carnegie, the great steel magnate. Much has been said and much has been written about Carnegie. Some of it has been derogatory. But let me tell you that during the course of a friendship that lasted through many years, I never knew a person of higher ideals, of warmer heart, or greater love for his fellow man.

Nowhere did he demonstrate this love more directly than in his suggestion that I take on the task of formulating a definite philosophy of human achievement. It was his hope that people such as you could avoid the haphazard trial-and-error method by which he rose to his high station.

As result of Mr. Carnegie's suggestion, and with his help, I spent twenty years interviewing hundreds of successful people in all walks of life.

Many of these people became my close personal friends. They included men such as Thomas Edison, Alexander Graham Bell, and Henry Ford.

Out of this research evolved what is known as the "science of success," based on seventeen principles which I found to be the deciding factors in bringing about an individual's success or failure.

Five Absolute Essentials of Success

Five of these principles will be presented to you today as absolute essentials of success. If properly applied, they can carry you from this point forward to wherever you desire to be in the calling of your choice.

I must remind you, however, that there is no such reality in this world as something for nothing. Everything worth having has a price upon it. As Emerson has so well stated: "Nothing can bring you peace but yourself. Nothing can bring you peace but the triumph of principles."

Paraphrasing this wise admonition, let us say that nothing can bring you success but yourself.

Nothing can bring you success but the application of the principles that have been responsible for all successes.

Let me list for you now the five essentials of success. They are:

1.   Definiteness of Purpose

2.   The Master Mind principle

3.   Going the Extra Mile

4.   Self-Discipline

5.   Applied Faith

Definiteness of Purpose

All successful achievement starts with definiteness of purpose. No man may hope to succeed unless he knows precisely what he wants and conditions his mind to complete the action necessary to attain it.

How does one go about conditioning his mind with definiteness of purpose? Simply by cultivating a deep and enduring capacity for belief!

I could cite example after example to prove that definiteness of purpose pays off. But I can think of no better case than that of Mr. W. Clement Stone of Chicago.

Shortly after my book *Think and Grow Rich* was published, Mr. Stone came across a copy of it. At that time, he was earning a modest living as an insurance salesman. That was in 1938.

As a result of what my book said about the need to choose a definite goal in life, Mr. Stone took a notebook from his pocket and wrote the following words: "My goal in life is this: By 1956 I will be president of the biggest exclusive old-line legal reserve health and accident insurance company in the world."

Mr. Stone signed his name to this and began reading it over to himself daily until it was seared into his consciousness. And because he knew what he wanted, he was able to recognize opportunity when it came his way. When the chance came for him to acquire the Combined Insurance Company of America, he was able to act with swift determination toward accomplishing his goal. And through his energy, the firm has now become what he determined it would be—the biggest exclusive accident and health firm in the world.

Now, I might add, Mr. Stone devotes much of his time and talent to helping others achieve their goals—by sponsoring the Science of Success home study course and by publishing a monthly magazine, *Success Unlimited.*

Mr. Stone became successful because he knew what he wanted, believed he would get it, and stood by that belief until it produced the opportunities he needed to fulfill his purpose.

There is something about the power of thought that seems to attract to a person the material equivalent of his aims and purposes. This power is not man-made. But it was made for man to use, and to enable him to control much of his earthly destiny.

In essence, we enter this world with the equivalent of a sealed envelope containing a long list of blessings each of us may enjoy by embracing and using the power of our minds. But the envelope also contains a list of penalties to be paid by the person who neglects to recognize this power and use it.

This gift is the only thing any of us controls absolutely. Therefore, it's the most precious thing we possess.

Just remember this: Whatever it is you possess, you must use it wisely—or lose it. And this, of course, includes your inexorable right to establish your own purpose in life and to keep your mind fixed on that purpose until you attain it.

Remember, also, that you can hit no higher than you aim. Therefore, don't be afraid to aim high—very high.

Which reminds me of the time the great evangelist, Dwight Moody, joined another minister in asking a wealthy lady for her contribution to a building fund. Before entering her mansion, Moody asked the other minister what amount they should request of the woman.

"Oh," said the pastor, "about $250."

"I think you'd better let me handle this," Moody replied.

When he met the lady, Moody said flatly: "We've come to ask you for two thousand dollars toward building a new mission."

The lady threw up her hands in horror and said: "Oh, Mr. Moody! I couldn't possibly give more than one thousand dollars."

Moody and the minister walked away with a check in that amount.

The point of this story, of course, is that life will give you young people no more than you demand of it. You may not achieve all that you hope to. But unless you choose a definite major purpose in life, you cannot hope to achieve *anything*!

Remember, too, that your goal need not involve the accumulation of material wealth.

Men like Albert Schweitzer, Jonas Salk, and Father Damien have achieved their definite major purposes. And in not one of these cases was it their purpose to acquire so much as a single dollar for the money itself. Indeed, I can think of no greater way for any of you to gain happiness and peace of mind during your lifetime than to set yourself a specific goal for serving your fellow human beings.

On the other hand, let me emphasize that there is no conflict between wealth and a state of spiritual peace of mind. Wealth, honestly acquired, is a great blessing—and especially so when the wealthy person thinks of himself as a steward who can use his funds to help others.

In selecting your goal, remember that nothing is impossible in this day when, as Rodgers and Hammerstein said in *Cinderella,* "Impossible things are happening every day."

As a news reporter, I covered the efforts of the Wright Brothers at Arlington, Virginia, to convince the Navy they had a machine that could fly.

For three days I sat in my automobile as Orville and Wilbur Wright endeavored to get their plane into the air. Finally, it rose for a few seconds, then came down with a crash and appeared broken to pieces.

An elderly gentleman standing nearby said: "They'll never make them thar things fly, will they, son? If God had wanted man to fly, he would have given him wings, wouldn't he?"

At the time, it appeared the old man was right. But I wonder what that gentleman would have said if, a few days ago, he could have sat with me in a modern airliner, flying at more than three hundred miles an hour, nearly five miles above the earth, calmly eating lunch?

How can you master the first of the five essentials of success?

Decide soon—within the next few weeks, if possible— upon a definite major purpose in your life. Write it down clearly and in detail in a pocket-sized notebook. Sign it, memorize it, and repeat it aloud at least three times daily in affirmation of your belief that it can be achieved.

In the same notebook, write out a clear description of the plan by which you intend to achieve your goal. State the maximum of time in which you intend to achieve it. Also, describe in detail precisely why you believe you will attain your purpose and what you intend to give in return for it. This latter is important. Give it much thought.

> **Keep your goal constantly before you.**

Keep your goal constantly before you so that your sub-conscious mind can work on it through auto-suggestion.

And above all, don't forget to seek guidance in prayer. Throughout your lifetime, your spirit must grow apace with your body. Prayer and work go hand in hand to bring us peace of mind.

This was illustrated when the head of a monastery heard a monk express doubt about the order's motto: "Pray and work." He invited the young man to go rowing with him and took the oars himself.

After a while, the young man pointed out that the superior was using only one oar and said: "If you don't use both, we'll just go around in circles and you won't get anywhere."

"That's right, my son," the elder man replied. "One oar is called prayer and the other is called work. Unless you use both at the same time, you just go in circles and you don't get anywhere."

The seasoning influence of the years on my life has brought me into a better understanding of the attitude in which to go to prayer. As a result, I now always close my prayer with these words:

> *Oh Infinite Intelligence, I ask not for more blessings, but more wisdom with which to make better use of the greatest of all blessings with which I was endowed at birth—the right to embrace and direct to ends of my own choice the powers of my mind.*

The Master Mind

This brings us to the second of the five essentials of success, known as the *Master Mind* principle. It consists simply of an alliance of two or more persons who coordinate their efforts in a spirit of perfect harmony for the attainment of a definite purpose.

It was Andrew Carnegie who first introduced me to this principle when I asked him to describe the means by which he had accumulated his great fortune. He answered frankly that it came through the efforts of other men—the men who belong to his Master Mind group. Then, one by one, he named the members of the group and what each contributed to its success.

Carnegie made clear to me that while *any* individual can achieve success, far greater success can be achieved through a group working in perfect harmony so that their talents, education, and personalities complement one another.

The Declaration of Independence was created by the most profound Master Mind alliance this nation has ever known. It consisted of the fifty-six brave men who signed the document, knowing that they were risking both their lives and their fortunes. Here was perfect harmony at its highest level—and its results have, to a large extent, changed the destiny of the entire human race.

There are three points of contact at which I urge you to relate yourself with others on the Master Mind basis: in your home, in your church, and in your place of occupation or business. Do this faithfully and you will have gone a long way toward insuring your prosperity, peace of mind, and sound health.

Time and again I have seen how the Master Mind alliance—the group working in harmony—produces astounding results.

Could one man, for example, ever have accomplished the scientific work that resulted in production of atomic power? Never! Each of us can accomplish only so much in a single lifetime. But by working in a harmony with others toward a single goal, results that normally would take centuries can be achieved in a relatively short time.

Going the Extra Mile

The third of the five essentials of success is the habit of *Going the Extra Mile*. In the Sermon on the Mount, we are told: "If any man requires you to go with him one mile, go with him twain."

The habit of going the extra mile merely means the practice of rendering more and better service than you are paid to render—and doing it in a positive, pleasing attitude.

I have never known a single person to achieve outstanding success without following the habit of rendering more service than was expected of him.

And I wish to cite you the record of a man whom I first met here at Salem College when I delivered the commencement address thirty-five years ago. He is a man who is well known to all of you. Of course, I'm speaking of Jennings Randolph, who, I should add, is known affectionately in my organization as "Mr. Courtesy."

After completing his work at Salem College, Jennings was elected to Congress, where he served the people of West Virginia for fourteen years. And I wish to tell you just one of the ways in which he followed the habit of going the extra mile.

During the summer, after Congress adjourned and most other congressmen had returned to their homes to attend to private affairs, Jennings remained at his office in

Washington, maintaining his staff as usual in order to be of continuous service to his constituents.

He didn't have to do this. It wasn't expected of him. Nor did he get extra pay for doing it—that is, no pay that came in his government paycheck.

All successful achievement starts with definiteness of purpose. No man may hope to succeed unless he knows precisely what he wants and conditions his mind to complete the action necessary to attain it.

But there came a day when this habit of going beyond the letter of responsibility began to pay off handsomely. This habit brought him to the attention of the president of Capital Airlines, who appointed him as assistant to the president and director of public relations for Capital.

Thirty-five years ago, Jennings Randolph heard me describe the benefits one may receive by going the extra mile when I delivered my first Salem College commencement address. He was impressed by what he heard. He was ready for the message. Then and there he declared his intention of embracing this principle and applying it in all of his human relationships.

Jennings Randolph has prospered and his friends are legion throughout this nation because he recognized that whatever we do to or for another, we do to or for ourselves—that no useful service can be rendered without its just reward, albeit the reward may not come back from the source to which we delivered the service.

"Men suffer all their life long," said Emerson, "under the foolish superstition that they can be cheated. But it is as impossible for a man to be cheated by anyone but himself, as for a thing to be, and not to be, at the same time. There is a third silent party to all our bargains. The nature and soul of things takes on itself the guaranty of fulfillment of every contract, so that honest service cannot come to loss. If you serve an ungrateful master, serve him the more. Every stroke shall be repaid. The longer the payment is withholding, the better for you; for compound interest on compound interest is the rate and usage of this exchequer."

When Paul Harris graduated from law school, he was confronted with the problem of building a clientele.

He had never heard of the principle of *Going the Extra Mile,* as such. But he put the principle to work so effectively that he lived to see the day when he turned away more prospective clients he could not serve than those he accepted.

His plan was simple. He invited a group of business and professional men to meet with him at luncheon weekly in what he called the Rotary Club. The original purpose of the club was to inspire its members to patronize one another and to induce outsiders to patronize members of the club.

The plan worked so successfully that Rotary is now an international institution with influences for the betterment of mankind all over the world. There is nothing to hinder you young men who contemplate entering a profession from adopting Paul Harris's principle and giving it an application that can increase your acquaintanceship and build goodwill for you as it did for him.

Self-Discipline

The fourth essential for success is *Self-Discipline*. That means mastery of self over both the mental faculties and the physical body. Self-discipline begins with a burning desire to become the master of one's self. The motivation necessary to keep that desire alert and active is recognition of the fact that when one becomes master of himself, he may become the master over many things—including the failures and defeats and problems that we encounter along the way.

Another inspiring motive that should keep the burning desire for self-mastery alive is recognition of the true significance of the gift from the Creator of one's unchallengeable right to control and direct his own mind.

Milo C. Jones worked a small farm near Fort Atkinson, Wisconsin. His hours were long, the work was hard, and every member of his family had to help in order to make ends meet.

Then disaster struck. Milo was stricken down by double paralysis and totally deprived of the use of his body. His farming days were over forever.

His family rolled him out in a wheelchair on the porch each day, where he sat in the sun while other members of the family carried on with the farmwork.

One morning, some three weeks after he was stricken, he made a stupendous discovery. He discovered that he had a mind.

Inasmuch as his mind was the only thing he had left with which he could exercise any sort of discipline, he began to put it to work. As a result, he came up with an idea that brought him and his family happiness and wealth.

Calling his family around him, he said, "I want you to plant every acre of our land in corn. Start raising hogs on this corn, and while they are still young and tender, slaughter them and make them into 'Little Pig Sausage.'"

"Little Pig Sausage" became a household word all over America, and Milo C. Jones lived to see his brainchild make him a very rich man. Although he learned very late, he made the discovery that I trust each of you young people will make early in your career: he discovered that there are no limitations to the power of the mind except those which one sets up for himself through doubts, fears, and lack of ambition or definiteness of purpose.

Your first duty in forming the habit of self-discipline is to try to win full and complete control of your own mind and direct it to definite objectives from which you may gain wisdom as well as material and spiritual prosperity.

Then you will need discipline over the emotion of anger. This you can attain by recognizing that no one can make you angry without your full consent and cooperation. You do not need to give that cooperation.

You will need discipline over your sex emotions, by learning the art of transmuting this profound creative force into channels that will aid you in the calling you have chosen.

You will need discipline over your tone of voice so as to make it gentle, yet convincing.

You will need discipline over everything you take into your physical body in the form of food, and drink, and drugs, and alcohol, and smokes. Remember, your body is God's temple, given you as a house for the protection of your mind and soul.

You will need discipline over your choice of personal associates.

You will need discipline over your thought habits, by keeping your mind busily occupied in thinking and planning for the things and circumstances you desire and off of those you do not desire.

You will need discipline to avoid procrastination.

You will need discipline over the emotion of love. If you love without your love being returned, be satisfied that *you* are the one who has gained most because the expression of love has added refinements to your soul. Therefore, don't waste time over unrequited love—and perish the idea that one can love but once.

You will need to discipline yourself to recognize that whatever happens to you, be it good or bad, most likely had its cause somewhere within you—either by your thoughts, deeds, or your neglect to act.

This is quite an order that I have given you.

But you can fill it if you are interested enough in your future to do so. By the time you will have filled this order you will know yourself, your potentials for success, your weaknesses, and your strengths. And you will be in a position to make the most of the prerogative your Creator has given you to control both your mind and your body.

Applied Faith

This brings us to the fifth and the last of the five essentials of success. It is called *Applied Faith*—the sort of faith that one backs with deeds as well as belief.

Faith is a state of mind that has been called "the mainspring of the soul," and it is that through which one's aims, desires, plans, and purposes may be translated into their material equivalent.

Faith begins with the recognition of the existence and the inexorable powers of Infinite Intelligence. There is no such reality as a blanket faith based upon an unproven hypothesis.

Faith is guidance! It won't of itself bring you the things you desire. But it can and will show you the path by which you may go after those things.

Through faith you can do anything you believe you can do, provided only that it harmonizes with natural laws.

When Dr. Frank W. Gunsaulus was a young preacher on Chicago's South Side, his following was small, his income meager. But he had long cherished the idea of building a new type of educational institution where the students would devote half their time to "book learning," the other half to applying this training in the laboratory of practical experience.

He needed a million dollars to start the project. So he asked for guidance through prayer. His efforts brought him immediate and dramatic results—an idea he believed would give him the money he needed.

He wrote a sermon entitled "What I Would Do with a Million Dollars" and announced in the Chicago newspapers that he would preach a sermon on that subject the following Sunday.

That Sunday morning, before he left his home for his church, he knelt down and offered the most fervent prayer he had ever expressed, requesting that the notice of his sermon would come to the attention of someone who could provide the money he sought.

Then he rushed to his church. As he was ascending the pulpit, however, he discovered that he had left his carefully prepared sermon at home—too far away to be recovered in time to deliver it.

"Right then and there," said Dr. Gunsaulus, "I offered another prayer, and in a matter of seconds, the answer I desired came. It said, 'Go into your pulpit and tell your audience of your plan, and tell it with all of your enthusiasm your soul can muster.'"

Dr. Gunsaulus did just that. He described the sort of school he had long wished to organize, how he wished to operate it, the sort of benefits it would render its students, and the amount of money he needed to get it going.

Those who heard the sermon said he never spoke like that before and never again thereafter, for he was speaking as an inspired man with a burning desire to render a great service.

At the end of his sermon, a stranger arose from the rear of the church, walked slowly down the aisle, whispered something in the minister's ear, then slowly walked back to his seat.

There was absolute silence.

Then Dr. Gunsaulus said, "My friends, you have just witnessed one of God's miracles. The gentleman who just walked down the aisle and spoke to me is Philip D. Armour. He told me if I would come down to his office, he would arrange for me to have the million dollars I need for the school."

The donation built the Armour School of Technology, of which Dr. Gunsaulus became the head. In recent years, the school has become part of the Illinois Institute of Technology.

"The mystery of the whole thing," said Dr. Gunsaulus, "was why I waited so long before going to the proper source for the solution of my problem."

That same mystery has confused many other people who have delayed going to prayer until after everything else had failed to bring the desired results in times of need and emergency.

And this may be one reason why prayer so often brings only negative results, as it generally does when one goes to prayer without true faith, after having met with disaster, or when disaster seems imminent.

I have received an impressive lesson on the power of prayer when my second son was born without ears.

The doctors broke the news to me as gently as possible, hoping to soften the shock. They ended the announcement by saying, "Of course, your son will always be a deaf-mute because no one born like him has ever learned to hear or to speak."

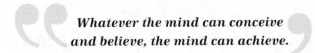

> *Whatever the mind can conceive and believe, the mind can achieve.*

There was a mighty fine opportunity for me to test my faith, and I did it by telling the doctors that while I had not seen my son, there was one thing of which I was very sure—that he would not go through life as a deaf-mute.

One of the doctors walked over, laid his hand on my shoulder, and said, "Now look here, Napoleon, there are some things in this world that neither you nor anyone else can do anything about, and this is one of them."

"There is nothing I can't do something about," I replied, "if it is no more than relate myself to an unfortunate circumstance so as to prevent it from breaking my heart."

I went to work on my son through prayer before I saw him, and I kept this up many hours daily. After three years, it became obvious that he was hearing. How much he heard we did not know.

But by the time he was nine years old he had developed sixty-five percent of his normal hearing capacity. That was enough to get him through the grade schools, high school, and to the third year in the University of West Virginia, when the Acousticon Company built him an electrical hearing aid that gave him his full, one hundred percent hearing capacity—just what I told the doctors would happen.

Out of that experience came my motto "Whatever the mind can conceive and believe, the mind can achieve." I wrote that motto literally in tears of sorrow, under emotional strain that tore at my heartstrings.

And somehow I can never dismiss the thought that this experience has been the richest of my entire life, because it brought me safely through a testing time from which I learned that our only limitations are those that we set up and accept in our minds.

I have now given you what I consider the five essentials of success. You may use them, if you choose to unlock the door to your desired goal in life.

Great as has been our scientific advances in the thirty-five years since I last appeared here, I look for still greater progress in the coming three-and-a-half decades. But these advances won't be in the field of science alone. They will be in the field of humanity itself.

A new spirit is sweeping the world in spite of the dark fears raised by the threat of nuclear warfare. Man is indeed learning that he is his brother's keeper! We are advancing not only in the material realm, but in the realm of the spirit. Never in the history of mankind have so many persons devoted their time and energy and wealth to helping other men and women.

There are no better goals for you young people than to join the ranks of these altruists.

Remember that we do not *find* happiness; we make it. And by like token, the things you sell for a price are gone forever, while the things you give away with your sincere blessings come back to you greatly multiplied.

Christianity has become one of the great forces of civilization because its founder paid for it with his life and gave it to the world with his blessings.

In the spirit of brotherly love, which he taught, I have brought you this message with the hope that it may help smooth the path of your lives and bring you nearer to your chosen goals.

Napoleon Hill spoke at a dental convention in 1952, at a time when he was in partial retirement. Hill was sixty-nine years old, and he seized upon the opportunity to lecture in Chicago.

In 1908, Hill had spent time interviewing the steel magnate Andrew Carnegie, who encouraged him to pursue his lifelong journey in developing the philosophy of success.

At the dental convention Hill was introduced by insurance tycoon W. Clement Stone. When a young man, Stone was given a copy of Hill's bestseller, *Think and Grow Rich,* and Stone was so impressed he gave away thousands of copies. Every person who came to work for Stone's insurance company received a copy.

Stone sat with Hill at the convention and challenged him to come out of semi-retirement to teach the philosophy of success. Hill agreed to Stone's request, provided that Stone would be Hill's general manager. A union of the two great men was planned for five years and lasted ten years. During this period Hill often used Stone as one of the finest examples of application of the philosophy of success.

Together, Hill and Stone gave lectures in many cities. Stone became immensely influential in Hill's personal life, assuring that Hill retired as a millionaire.

Hill and Stone jointly wrote *Success Through a Positive Mental Attitude* in 1960, and it became an immediate best seller. Over fifty years later, the book still sells well in the United States and all over the world.

"Maker of Miracle Men" is the result of Hill's work with Stone. Prefacing the speech is the excellent introduction that Stone gave Hill.

—DON GREEN

Introduction by W. Clement Stone to
Maker of Miracle Men

by
Napoleon Hill

I'll tell you of a few miracles this evening for one purpose and one purpose only: because there is someone in this audience—there is someone whose life tonight is going to be affected for the better. Otherwise, Dr. Hill and I are wasting our time and you yourself are wasting your time, because the science of success philosophy gets men to act.

In 1940, I was holding a sales meeting in Salt Lake City. Before the meeting, I walked down the main street, and as I was coming back to the Utah Hotel, I passed a coal store. In the window was a chunk of coal about four feet high, four feet in cube, and in front of that chunk of coal was a book. The name of the book was *Think and Grow Rich*.

Now, after that book was given to me back in 1938, I had subsequently given away thousands of those books free of cost. And, as I say, I saw miracles performed. So I went into the store and asked for the owner. If any of you are from Salt

Lake City or have been out there, perhaps you remember the coal store, Martin's Coal Store.

I asked Mr. Martin why he put a book in front of a chunk of coal, and I explained how I had used the book: how it had helped individuals solve their personal problems, how it had helped them solve their financial problems, how it had helped individuals, when they got to a spot when there was no way to turn, turn that liability into an asset. Or, using Napoleon Hill's phraseology: "With every adversity there's a seed of an equivalent benefit." And they took advantage of that situation and were happy that they encountered that experience.

So, Mr. Martin said to me, "I'm going to tell you something that I would never tell a stranger. I don't believe you're a stranger because we have so much in common." He said, "A few years ago, my partner and I had two businesses (the coal business and a gravel business), and both were in the red. We thought we could save one by selling the other, and we found that we couldn't. And by some chance, I was given a book—this book, *Think and Grow Rich*." And he said, "Within the last few years—and," he said, "this is what I wouldn't tell a stranger—both businesses got out of the red. And today, with all of our bills paid, we show cash assets, in addition to our inventory, of $186,000." And he pulled out his bankbook to show me.

Well, a year ago last August I had given a talk before the Kiwanis Club—North Shore Kiwanis Club—at the Edgewater Beach Hotel in Chicago on the book *Think and Grow Rich*. And as was my custom, I gave some of the books away, particularly to individuals who I thought were ready. One was to a young dentist, Dr. Herbert Gustafson. A month later, Dr. Gustafson telephoned me and asked if I'd like to meet Napoleon Hill. He mentioned that he was giving a talk before a study group, a group of dentists here in Chicago. I was very thrilled because I had thought that Dr. Hill had passed away. Fortunately, I found that he was very much alive.

I went to the meeting, and at the noonday luncheon I was placed next to Dr. Hill. We discussed philosophy, and I suggested that, in view of the success of such movies as the Bettger film *How I Raised Myself from Failure to Success in Selling*, that he come out with a movie on *Think and Grow Rich*. We talked for a while, and then it was suggested that he return to Chicago and we explore the possibility.

After two or three days, Dr. Hill, at my advice, agreed to come out of retirement for a period of five years. He agreed to do it on one condition—that I would be his general manager. And that is the reason I am here tonight.

Mr. Allen told you about Napoleon Hill Associates. There's only one justification for it—just one—and that is to spread the philosophy of American achievements as taught to Napoleon Hill by Andrew Carnegie.

Now, during the past year—and that's when the associates have been operating, the period of time which we've been operating—we have actually seen miracles performed. In my own business, I've seen mediocre salesmen become super salesmen. Men who were earning, say, $125 per week raised their incomes up to three, four, and five hundred dollars a week—in other words, performing the impossible.

In our classes, for example—and I see that we have some of our students here this evening—in our night classes, for example, we have helped individuals by encouraging and inspiring them to help themselves. It's so easy to solve a problem—it's so easy to solve it intelligently—if you know how.

> *Dr. Hill's writings...crystallize the science of success into a simple, understandable formula that Mr. Average Man, or Mrs. Average Woman, or any young high-school boy or girl can follow.*

The wonderful thing about Dr. Hill's writings, as Earl Nightingale told me, is that they crystallize the science of success into a simple, understandable formula that Mr. Average Man, or Mrs. Average Woman, or any young high-school boy or girl can follow.

Let me tell just one or two stories about some of our students. The one that impresses me at the moment is one about a young chap whose last name is Gromeyer; maybe some of you know him. He's a teacher of music. In about the third week in the seventeen weeks of the course, he took fifteen minutes of the time of the class to prove that it was impossible for a teacher of music to earn more than one hundred dollars per week.

Well, when I'm in a class with this type of group, my theory is I'd rather have one person solve his problem permanently than coast along and maybe have no problem solved, so we worked on him for about an hour. I have a letter from Mr. Gromeyer. In the letter, he apologizes for not attending our last few classes. He says, "First, it might interest you to know I can sleep much better. I'm not as nervous as I used to be." He says, "I shall forever be indebted to the Napoleon Hill Associates." He says, "You remember when I pointed out that it was impossible, before I understood the philosophy, for a teacher of music to earn more than one hundred dollars a week?" He said, "It might interest you to know that in the last ten weeks, my average income was between $375 and $385 a week."

Well, I could give you story after story of what is happening in our classes. Now, why do I tell you this? Because when Napoleon Hill and I agreed to a five-year program, we decided that we were going to do fifty years' work in five, ten—in one. To do that, we must have many Napoleon Hills. We must have many teachers. We must have many moderators. And we must organize so that this philosophy will go to everyone who chooses to receive it.

There is not a day during the business week but what someone comes into my office from far parts of the country or even from far parts of the world. A man was in my office, flew in from Rome this past week—a man who is teaching the philosophy to Europeans, to Asians, to Africans, the philosophy so contrary to the philosophy of the high-caste, low-caste system, which is contrary to the American philosophy, the philosophy whereby the individual can accomplish anything that he conceives and believes.

If you do nothing else tonight but memorize that slogan and burn indelibly in your memory the phrase "conceive, believe, and achieve," and you believe it, you will walk away with a power whereby you can accomplish anything in life you choose to accomplish. And you take a country, when someone gets before these people and points out that the individual has an inherent power, a power whereby God has given him the right to do that which his mind conceives he can do, you can see how those of us who are trying to help others help themselves get the joy and thrill out of our work.

Now, there is an expression that I use regarding Napoleon Hill. You judge for yourself whether it is warranted. I could take your time all evening, give you story after story as to why I call him "Napoleon Hill, maker of miracle men." If you are ready, listen. Listen carefully and take away with you the message he will try to give you. Thank you.

Maker of
Miracle Men

by
Napoleon Hill

Good evening, ladies and gentlemen. You know, people are wonderful, if you come to know them properly. And one of the things about the work that I'm engaged in is that I am bringing people together under the proper circumstances, where they find out the better qualities of each other.

Inasmuch as I'm dividing up my talk into three nights, inasmuch as I contemplate becoming well acquainted with some of you, I'm going to take you back to the beginning of all of this movement now that it's spreading all over the world. I'm going to take you back to that log cabin down in the mountains of Southwest Virginia—in Wise County, to be exact—to that little one-room log shack where I was born quite a long while ago. Not as long as you may think, however.

I remember so well the equipment that they had in that house. It had one table, which was fastened to the wall in such a way by hinges that you could let it down when not in use. It had one bed, one mattress made up of chopped-up shucks. It wasn't anything like the inner-spring mattresses we have today. They had one big oven in which they baked bread over the fire. They owned one horse and one cow and one ham, donated to them by their respective parents. That's the way my father and my mother started out.

And when I came along, I was born to a heritage of the four horsemen: poverty, fear, superstition, and illiteracy. Now, theoretically speaking, ladies and gentlemen, there wasn't a chance on the face of this earth of my ever escaping the confines of Wise County, where I was born, down in that part of the country that was famous for three things—corn liquor, rattlesnakes, and mountain feuds—until a very marvelous thing happened: my mother died, and my father brought into the home, eventually, a new mother, by far and away the most wonderful person I have ever known in my entire life.

The Science of Success

She was wonderful on account of the influence that she had upon me at a time when I needed good influences. And now for the benefit of you dentists, I'm going to tell you what a resourceful woman my stepmother was. She was making application of this philosophy of the science of a success back in those days, and I didn't know it; I didn't recognize it as such. My stepmother had a set of artificial teeth, an upper plate. At that time, I didn't know there were such things; I'd never seen a denture previously.

I've found out a lot about them since. One morning she was getting breakfast, and she dropped this plate and broke it. My father went over and picked up the pieces and assembled them in his hand, and he looked at them for a few moments. He said, "Martha, you know, I believe I can make a set of teeth." She dropped her pots and pans, and ran over there, and grabbed him around the neck, and hugged and kissed him, and said, "Well, I know you could make a set of teeth." Well, I thought, "My, oh my, what a woman!

My old man make a set of teeth? I know he could shoe a horse; I've seen him do that. But make a set of teeth? Well, that's ridiculous. Where would he get the bone, anyhow, to make the teeth?"

Well, anyhow, a little while later I came home from school, and I smelled a peculiar odor when I got up in the yard. When I got inside the house, I saw a queer little kettle sitting over the fire. I asked my stepmother what it was. She said, "That is a vulcanizer. Your father sent away; we got all of this here equipment. He made an impression of my mouth this morning. He made me a set of teeth, and they're in there cooking."

Well, by and by they took the little kettle off the fire and took it down to the river to cool it down so they could take out this hunk of Plaster of Paris. My father took his knife and peeled the Plaster of Paris away, and then he took a horse rasp—I don't know whether you know what a horse rasp is or not. I don't know whether you know what a horse is anymore or not. A horse rasp is a course file with which you cut away the surplus part of the hoof after you put the shoe on—he took this up to the fine end of this horse rasp and cut off the surplus rubber of this plate, and then took a piece of emery cloth and rubbed it down and put it in my mother's mouth. And believe it or not, dentists, it fit almost perfectly.

And then my father started practicing dentistry. He went down to the blacksmith shop, and he made himself a pair of forceps. He made himself a little instrument, which he called an "engine," which he worked with his foot for drilling purposes. And he set out on horseback across the mountains of Virginia, Tennessee, and Kentucky practicing dentistry, and just in no time we were in the money.

This had been going on for about three years, and one day the JP came down with a big law book under his arm. And he said, "Look here, Dr. Hill, it says here at 506 and 540 of the Code of Virginia that you can't practice dentistry without a license, and if you do, you're liable to go to jail." Well, my father went out to the county seat to see what could be done about it. And when he came back, I saw him riding up the valley, and I knew he had been defeated. He got off the horse, and he said, "Well, Martha, it's all off. I can't be a dentist anymore. I find that I have to take an examination, and, of course, you know I couldn't do that." And she said, "Look here, Dr. Hill, I didn't make a dentist out of you to have you let me down. Now, if you have to take an examination, you'll take it just like everybody else. You'll go away to college." And I thought to myself, "What a woman! What a woman! My old man go away to college? Why, they wouldn't let him on the campus ground, let alone inside."

Ladies and gentlemen, she sent him down to Louisville Dental College for four years. He took every medal that was offered down there for the first year, and they wouldn't let him compete the fourth year because they knew he would win it. You see, he was a better dentist when he went there than most of them were when they left. And she paid for his tuition by using the life insurance money of her former husband.

Now ladies, I hope I've given you, in that illustration, a sample of what you can do to put your husband across if you really and truly do it—and I don't mean to be facetious in making that suggestion. I think perhaps one of the grandest things that can be done with this philosophy is show the wives to take an interest in it and inspire their husbands to make use of it.

And now, this wonderful woman, who made a dentist out of my father, took me in hand. She said, "Now, you're the eldest in the family. We got to find out what you're going to do." And then we finally wound up by her influencing me to become a newspaper writer. We, at one time, were corresponding for about sixteen different newspapers—small county papers.

And on days when there was no news, I made news, believe me—and some of it was really dramatic: mountain feuds, moonshiners, revenuers. I'll tell you, we had lots of material to work off of. And one day I described in one of my stories a raid on a neighbor's farm, and I described it so perfectly that it turned out that there was a still there. The revenuers came, and they had missed the still by about thirty minutes. And the farmer came over and put my father on notice that that lad of his, if he did any more writing about moonshine stills, he'd have to get out of the county. That was the last story I wrote about moonshining.

Out of that newspaper experience, ladies and gentlemen, came the ability that finally got me my opportunity with the great philosopher-philanthropist-industrialist Andrew Carnegie.

My brother and I had matriculated to Georgetown University Law School intending to become lawyers. We didn't have any money, but I did have the ability to write. And I promised that I would write stories about successful men, sell them to a magazine, and then pay our way through. And my first assignment, fortunately, was with Andrew Carnegie in Pittsburgh. He gave me three hours. And when the three hours were over, he said, "Now, this interview is just the beginning. Come on out to the house, stay all night, and after dinner we'll take up the interview again." He kept me there three days and nights—and believe you me, I was more than flattered. I wondered what it was all about.

A Common-Folk Economic Philosophy

He kept talking to me about the need for a new philosophy. He said, "We've had many philosophies from the days of Socrates and Plato on down to the days of William James and Emerson. But most of them deal with the moral laws of life. What we need is an economic philosophy for the man of the streets that will enable him to make use of the knowhow gained by men like myself over a lifetime of experience."

Well, it sounded very nice to me, except for one thing: I didn't know exactly what that word *philosophy* meant. And finally, at the end of the third day he said, "Now look here, I have been talking to you for three days about the need for a new philosophy. I'm going to ask you a question about it: If I commission you to become the author of this philosophy, give you letters of introduction to men whose experiences you will need in collaboration with yourself, are you willing to put in twenty years of research—because that's how long it will take—paying your own way as you go along, without any subsidy from me? Yes or no?"

Ladies and gentlemen, there have been many times in my life when I have faced difficult problems and difficult decisions, but I don't think I ever faced one more embarrassing than that, because when Mr. Carnegie put that proposition to me, my hand was down in my pocket and I was fiddling with the money that I had there—just about enough to get back to Washington. And if I'd had to stay at a hotel instead of Mr. Carnegie's house, I wouldn't have had that much. I didn't even know the meaning of the word *philosophy*, and here the richest man in the world wanted me to go to work for him for twenty years without pay. Wasn't that a situation for you?

I started to tell Mr. Carnegie...I started to do just exactly what you, or most of us people, would have done under the same circumstances. Now what do you think that was?

What would you have done if you had faced that sort of a proposition—going to work for twenty years without any pay for the richest man in the world?

Well, yes, that's what I was about to do. But something inside of me wouldn't let me open my mouth, until I got a hunch that if Mr. Carnegie had kept me there for three days, it must have been for a purpose. Now, he must have seen something in me that I didn't know was there. Also, this man, a man with Mr. Carnegie's reputation for picking men, certainly didn't pick me to do a job like that unless he knew I had the ability to do it. And whatever this something was, this silent, invisible person who was standing, looking over my shoulder, and whispering in my ear—said, "Go ahead and tell him 'yes.'"

I said, "Mr. Carnegie, I not only will accept the commission, sir, but you may depend upon it that I will complete it." He said, "I like the way you ended that sentence, and I think you'll do it. You have the job." The only contribution Mr. Carnegie ever made to me outside of introducing me when I needed to be introduced was to pay my expenses in the early part of my relationship with him.

The first man he sent me to see was Henry Ford. He said, "I want you to go up to Detroit and become acquainted with Henry Ford. Observe him carefully because one of these days, he's going to dominate the motor industry and he's going to be second only to the steel industry."

This was in 1908—the late fall of 1908, ladies and gentlemen. I went up there and spent two days so I could find Ford, and when I did, by then, he came out of the rear of a shop where he had been doing some experimenting with an old pair of overalls on, a plug hat or a derby hat that had been bashed in at the crown, grease all over his hands. I remember he got my shirtsleeves dirty when I shook hands with him. And I sat down for a half hour with Mr. Ford, and about all of his conversation consisted of "yes" and "no"— mostly "no." And I wondered how a man like Mr. Carnegie could have made a mistake like that, imagining Mr. Ford would ever be a leader in anything. Well, I won't tell you the rest of it; that's enough.

Now, since that time I've had the privilege of entering the lives of a great number of men in a great number of walks of life, of knowing their faults and their virtues, their failures and their mistakes. And in 1928, just exactly twenty years from the time Mr. Carnegie commissioned me, I interpreted in writing, in eight volumes, the first interpretation of the philosophy under the title of *The Law of Success*. It was published in Meriden, Connecticut, and it was distributed throughout the world.

I later on wrote *Think and Grow Rich*, which does not contain the entire philosophy, and that was distributed throughout the world. Through the aid and cooperation of the late Mahatma Gandhi in India, all of my books have been published in India, millions of them sold there. They have been published in the Portuguese language and distributed throughout Brazil. Millions of them have been sold in a special edition throughout the British Empire. And, all in all, I would say that there has never been an author any time in the history of the world, in any field, that had as much practical help as I've had in refining and perfecting the science of success and in taking it to the people.

To me, ladies and gentlemen, the most profound thing about this experience is, here I was a youngster, little education, no money—I never did have any backing or any organization back of me until a year ago, when Mr. W. Clement Stone took over. And despite all of that, on the merit of the philosophy alone it spread throughout this world and has benefited millions of people. And I just want to thank you. Thank you very much.

And I just want to tell you one thing so that you will not get the impression that I'm telling you what a smart man I am: I just want to tell you that that could not have been accomplished had there not been invisible powers guiding and directing me. You know that, and I know it.

You're as Crazy as Hell

Well, after I got through with my interview with Mr. Carnegie, I went back down to Washington and told my brother what had happened. He sat silently and never said a word until I told him the whole story. Then he got up, and he walked over, he put his hands on my shoulder, pulled me over close to him, and he said, "Napoleon, ever since you and I were little barefooted boys wading down in Guest River in Wise County, I have always suspected there was something wrong with you. But," he said, "from here on out, I never will suspect you again because I know now you're as crazy as hell." I'm quoting my brother.

And I want to tell you, ladies and gentlemen, that the time he was speaking—because I had gotten away from Mr. Carnegie and the influence of his great personality had worn off; I was down to the bare realities of life again—I want to tell you that my brother's words seemed like they had a lot of logic to them. And then I was only to meet with rebuff after rebuff. There wasn't a single, solitary one of my relatives who didn't agree with my brother's evaluation of what I had done. There was only one person among my friends and among my relatives that stood by me and said, "You can do it, and you will do it," and that was my stepmother. And when I tell you that, you know why I say she was the most wonderful woman I have ever known. But there have been two truly great women in my life—two. One was my stepmother, and the other is my wife, my alter ego, the one who is my greatest critic and yet my best friend. And to those two women I owe all that I have ever done of benefit to others, all that I shall ever do in the future.

Now, ladies and gentlemen, I'm going to give you some illustrations of the application of this philosophy, and I'll tell you what I'd like for you to do: Take this folder that you have there and open it up, and you will find that there are six of the seventeen principles of success that are outlined there. And as I give you each of these examples, I want you to observe how many of these six principles were made use of by the case histories that I'm now going to give you.

You'll notice that the first principle of success is that of *Definiteness of Purpose*. That's number one. Nobody ever achieved anything in this world worth achieving without definiteness of purpose. And I have reference to an overall major purpose. You may have, of course, minor purposes, but if you're going to be a success in life, you've got to aim for something in the future, something that you have not yet attained and something that represents what would, to you, be a successful life.

And number two is the principle of *Going the Extra Mile*. Now that means rendering more service and better service than you're paid to render, doing it all the time and doing it in a pleasing, pleasant mental attitude—you know, like everybody is doing today. Yeah, are they? Do you know, seriously, ladies and gentlemen, that the greatest sin of the age in which we are living right now is that the majority of people not only don't go the second mile; bless your lives, they don't even go the first one. And if they can do it, they get on the government subsidy payroll and don't want to do anything. Don't quote me on that 'cause somebody might think I'm in politics, which I'm not. But that does happen to be the truth, refusal to do a day's work for a day's pay—is one of the yields of our economy today, beyond any question of doubt.

This country was built by pioneers, by men who took chances, by men who went on their own initiative, by men who had courage, by men who were not afraid. And that's the kind of men and women that I'm trying to build with this philosophy—the type of people who created this great nation in which we live.

And the third principle is that of the *Master Mind*. The *Master Mind* principle means an alliance of two or more minds working in perfect harmony for the attainment of a definite objective. Now, the key words there are *perfect harmony*. There are many alliances working toward a definite objective, but unless that element of perfect harmony is there, the alliance is nothing more than cooperation or coordination of effort.

And the fourth principle is that of *Applied Faith*. I don't think I need to comment much on the meaning of that because you surely know it—applied faith, however, and not theoretical faith.

And the fifth principle is that of *Self-Discipline*. And the sixth one is *Cosmic Habitforce*. The law of cosmic habitforce is the comptroller of the natural laws of this universe, the shaper and the maker of all habits. And one of the queer things about man is that he is the only creature upon the face of this earth that has been given the power to break the hold of cosmic habitforce and make his own habits what he wants them to be. Every other creature, lower again in intelligence than man, comes into this world plain bounded by a pattern it can never break out of, a pattern called *instinct*. Man makes his own patterns. He can decree his own destiny. He can shape his own future. He can make his own job. And when you read that book *How to Raise Your Own Salary*, let me tell you that that title is not an overstatement of the truth; it's an understatement—because it is literally true that by following the formula laid out in that book, a man can raise his own salary, or a woman can raise her own salary, or set his position in life pretty much what he wants it to be.

I think if there was ever a time in this country when men and women need to recognize the power of their own minds, when they need to overcome frustration and fear, that time is now. There is too much fear spread around, too many people talking about depressions. We're trying very hard to see if we can't work ourselves into a depression or to see if we can't work ourselves into another world war. Let's get our minds, each and every one of us as individuals, fixed upon a definite goal so big and so outstanding that we'll have no time to think about these things we don't want.

Do you know that one of the queer things about mankind's existence is the fact that the vast majority of people are born, grow up, struggle, go through life in misery and in failure, never getting out of life what they want, not recognizing that it would be just as easy by the turn of a hand, so to speak, to switch over and get out of life exactly what they want, not recognizing that the mind attracts the thing that the mind dwells upon? You can think about poverty, you can think about failure, you can think about defeat—and that's exactly what you'll get. You can think about success, you can think about opulence, you can think about achievement—and that's what you'll get.

Mental and Spiritual Immunity

I want to tell you that the most difficult period of my life was in those twenty years between 1908 and 1928 when I had to give myself mental and spiritual immunity against the people who were saying, "You can't do it," "It can't be done," "You'll never live long enough." At least half of my energy went to resisting the people who thought it couldn't be done.

In fact, some years ago, a group of my students, on my birthday, got together a fund and bought me a nice dictionary—a nice large one. And the first thing I did—they rolled it out on the stage and gave it to me with a formal presentation—I took out my penknife and walked over, and I said, "Ladies and gentlemen, I thank you for your thoughtfulness, but I can't accept that book with one word that's in it because that one word is very offensive to me." And I turned over to the word *impossible* and clipped it right out. I said, "Now I'll accept the book, but I don't want any book that has the word *impossible* in it because I've seen the impossible happen so many times that I know there is no such thing."

How many of you know or have heard of Earl Nightingale's program? How many? Oh my, Earl has some friends here too.

I had one of the most joyous visits with Earl Nightingale about a year ago that I've ever had with anybody in Chicago in recent years. He sat down, and he told me a most dramatic story about what happened when he got a hold of my philosophy. He was working alone at an ordinary salary, not getting anywhere and very discouraged, when somebody put a copy of one of my books in his hand. And he went to bed and started reading it in bed, and all of a sudden, he got an idea out of that book that caused him to yell to his wife to come quickly—he'd found it. And she ran in, thought something had happened, and sure enough, she said, "You found what?"

"Why," he said, "I have found what I have been looking for so long, and I've found the thing that's standing between me and success." He said, "I went down the next day, and I made up my mind that I was going to put Napoleon Hill and his philosophy to a test. I made up my mind I was going to double my salary and I was going to do it that week. Well," he said, "believe you me, it was the easiest thing I ever did in my life. I only had to ask, and it was done."

And he said, "That almost scared me. I waited a little while, and I thought I'd try it again just to see if that wasn't a coincidence. And it worked again." Well, Earl doesn't have to worry now about raising his own salary; he's doing all right. He's on top, he's doing a grand job, and he's found himself. He's found Earl Nightingale. He's got his mind on the things he wants in life and not on the things he doesn't want. Ladies and gentlemen, that's all any of us needs. You know, it's not more knowledge, it's not more education we need, and it's not more facts. It's a better use of what we already have that we need to have.

You have, each and every one of you, within your own potential powers, now, you have everything necessary to do a wonderful job in your own chosen field if you would only embrace it and use it. Did you know, ladies and gentlemen, that when we are born, when we come over to this plane, we bring with us two sealed envelopes? In one of those sealed envelopes is a long list of the rewards and riches you may have for taking possession of your own mind and using it. And in another sealed envelope is an equally long list of the penalties you must pay if you don't embrace your own mind and use it.

The Creator didn't intend for men to be in possession of this marvelous, profound gift of thought without using it. And as some philosopher said—I wish I had said it, but I didn't: "Whatever it is that you have, you use it or you lose it." And that's just as applicable to your brainpower or your thinking power as it is to anything else. You'll use it or you'll lose it.

Just forty years ago, I came to Chicago for the first time. I lived here for ten years. I became the advertising manager of the La Salle Extension University—the first advertising manager they ever had. And I hadn't been there very long, about three months, until I found out that La Salle owed about everybody and had no money. And I wasn't sure, when I got my paycheck, that it would be recognized when I got to the bank, so I formed a habit of running over to the bank ahead of the others and having my check certified. Well, I got tired of that, and then I remembered what Mr. Carnegie had so often told me. He said, "When you have a problem, break it up into many parts and solve the problem a part at a time." So I made an inventory, thoroughly, of La Salle and found out what was wrong: they had a man in charge of the collection department who was something of a Simon Legree, threatening the students with punishment if they didn't pay their bills and making them all mad, and they weren't paying.

I induced the school to get that man another job with another company. That's just putting it rather mildly. And we put in his place a salesman who wrote nice letters to the students, and we did two things that put La Salle on top of the heap and kept it there for years. First of all, we took those students into partnership with the school and sold them some eight percent preferred stock, made partners of them. Secondly, we made agents out of them, and they started not only to pay up their own accounts, but they started to bring in their friends and enroll them in the courses. And La Salle had the fastest growth, I should say, for the following five years of any school at any time, anywhere.

If I hadn't have had this training under Mr. Carnegie, I wouldn't have known how to take a hold of that problem and break it up into its component pods. I had another opportunity to demonstrate the practicability of this philosophy before I was twenty-one years of age. I married and went down to the little town of Lumberport, West Virginia, to visit my in-laws. They had never seen me, and my wife took me down to show me off. And before we left Washington, I bought myself a nice outfit of clothes, got ready to make a good impression. But when we got down to Lumberport—or rather Haywood, two miles from Lumberport, where the interurban electric line stops, where you're supposed to be met by a horse-drawn carriage, it was raining hard and there was no carriage. And I had to walk over those two miles and carry two suitcases. And when I got over there, my nice outfit of clothes was spoiled—and also my disposition.

That was very fortunate because what happened enabled me to make what turned out to be worth very much more than a million dollars, and I did it in less than six months by my first application of the Carnegie philosophy. I said to my brothers-in-law, "Why don't you have the streetcar company build a spur line over here so you can get in and out of Lumberport without wading through the mud?" They said, "Well, did you see that big Monongahela River over there that you just crossed?" I said, "Yes." He said, "That's the reason why we don't." And he said, "We've been trying for ten years to get a streetcar built over, and we can't get one." I said, "Ten years? Well, I can do it in six months." And one of them said, "Well, that's fine, and we've really got somebody in the family now, haven't we?"

The rain had stopped by that time, and I asked my brothers-in-law to walk over to this river that was giving the trouble. And they told me that it would cost one hundred thousand dollars to build a bridge across that river and that was more than the streetcar company was willing to put into the entire project. I was standing there kind of stalling for a way out of that unfortunate misuse of my tongue. And here was a description of the river: The river—the banks of the river—were about one hundred feet high, and the county road went zigzagging down this side of the bank, and across a little rickety bridge, and up the other side of the bank, and then across about fourteen railroad-switching tracks. It was a place where the B&O Railroad came and made up their coal trains.

And while I was standing there, as is so often the case in an emergency, that man that stood looking over my shoulder—that silent person who stood there so many times when I had faced real problems that I couldn't have solved myself—he whispered in my ear, said, "You see that farmer down there that's waiting for that coal train to brake the train and open up the public highway?" A train had come along and blocked the highway. And I said to myself, "Yes, I see that, and I also see the solution. I see three parties that want this road, this bridge. The B&O Railroad Company wants that county road off of their tracks because one of these days they're going to have an accident there that will cost them many times the cost of the bridge.

"The county commissioners want the county road off of there for the same reason, and the streetcar company wants it off of there because they'd like to have some extra revenue coming out of Lumberport."

Inside of a week's time I had the names of the three parties—the B&O Railroad Company, the county commissioners, and the street railway company—on the dotted line. And at the end of the six-month period, I rode the first streetcar into Lumberport that ever went into that town.

Sometime later in 1934, I rode the last one out when they took up those tracks and provided them with buses.

Resourcefulness

Now, Mr. Carnegie taught me how to make this philosophy to cause you to become resourceful in a time of an emergency. And I want to tell you that I think that's one of the finest things that it does. When you're up against a stone wall, when you've exhausted all of your intelligence and all of your experience, when you've done everything that you know there, then this philosophy seems to come to the rescue and give you the answer. And I've seen it happen so many times it's not funny anymore.

In this very city, shortly after I came here as advertising manager of La Salle Extension University, I met Edwin C. Barnes, the only partner that Thomas Edison ever had. And Ed Barnes and I were over at the Sheraton Hotel having lunch or dinner, and he was telling me about his association with Mr. Edison. He was telling me how he went up to West Orange, New Jersey, on a freight train because he didn't have money enough to pay his way and sold Edison on taking him into partnership with him; how he had stood by for five years in one menial job after another, waiting for the opportunity to come, when he could become a partner of the great Edison.

And then he said something to me that I thought was in the way of boasting: he said, "Well, now that I'm doing all right, I'm making over twelve thousand dollars a year." I said, "Twelve thousand dollars a year? If I was a partner of the great Edison, I'd be making at least fifty thousand dollars a year." And he said, "How?" Have you ever thought of the importance of that word *how* when somebody is making a statement that you don't believe exactly can be backed up? Have you ever tried using that word *how*? Oh, I've seen them wiggle and squirm when that word was shot at them at the right time. And I did a little wiggling and squirming when Ed Barnes said, "How?" Well, then I became serious. I started in to apply the Carnegie philosophy. I started to ask questions, and by the time we were through eating, I had the plan that did the trick.

I had Ed Barnes form an exchange bureau made up of all of his salesmen and all of the salesmen of the typewriter companies and the salesmen of office supplies and desks in and near the Chicago territory. And through this bureau, when one of Barnes's men selling a dictating machine would find somebody who needed a desk or office supplies, he'd phone it into the bureau, and the bureau would transfer it over to the right salesman. And the salesmen in that field, when they heard of somebody who wanted a dictating machine, they'd phone into the bureau, and Barnes's men would get it. In other words, they were getting, with Barnes having in a little while about 150 salesmen, good leads and prospects without having to pay them anything.

It was something like during World War I when the price of fur became very high and a very shrewd German friend of mind started a cat farm. Well, he ran into a problem right away: he found out that the price of feed was also high. But being a student of this philosophy, he was shrewd enough to solve that problem, so he started a rat farm right along beside the cat farm. He fed the rats over to the cats, and he skinned the cats and fed part of the carcasses back to the rats; and that way he didn't have any feed bill anymore.

Well, my plans for Barnes were something like that. He had no expense. The first year after that happened, his income was over $50,000, the second one over $100,000, the third one over $150,000, and after that I never did get the figures; and I doubt that Uncle Sam did, either. But this much I know about Ed Barnes—he was up here last summer and visited with me. I had a nice visit with him. He lives down in Bradenton, Florida. He's retired—he's a multimillionaire, and he owes it all to this philosophy, every bit of it.

It has been said that I have made more successful men than any man living today. I don't know whether that's true or not because there's no way of getting accurate statistics. But, ladies and gentlemen, when I take inventory of the people that I do know who started at scratch and have become millionaires—and some of them not quite that much money, but have become profoundly successful—I recognize that I have created a philosophy here through the good work of Mr. Carnegie, who's been a benefactor to the world—not only to those who are living now, but to those who are not yet born.

When Mr. Carnegie sold me on organizing this philosophy, he said, "I'm going to give away my money before I die, as fast as I can find ways and means of giving it away without doing damage." And, as you of course know, he did just that. He gave it away for educational purposes, to libraries, to foundations for the maintenance of peace, and in every way that he could conceive. But he said, "By far, the greatest part of my riches I am entrusting to you to take to the people of the world in the form of the knowhow through which I gained my money." And he said, "If you carry through the trust and perfect your job, as I sincerely believe you will, you'll live to see the time when you're far and away richer than I am and when you will have made many more successful men than I have ever made."

And, ladies and gentlemen, when Mr. Carnegie made that statement, it was just too much for me to swallow. I thought, "Well, Mr. Carnegie has never flattered me before. He's never said anything that didn't turn out to be right. But that's just one of those things that never could happen." I have already made thousands of times more successful men than Mr. Carnegie ever has—thousands of times—and I'm still in the process of making them.

Profound Facts and Truths

You know, ladies and gentlemen, during those twenty years of research that I put into the building of this philosophy, I ran into some very profound facts and truths. And one of them consists in this fact: that when a great crisis comes over the world, there always comes out some unknown with a formula for dissolving that crisis—like Abraham Lincoln, for instance, in a time of need, when this country was about to be split asunder by internal strife; by George Washington, preceding Lincoln; by Franklin D. Roosevelt, at a time when the people were stampeded with fear and they were standing in great lines to draw their money out of the bank.

And I sometimes wonder if this hand of destiny, which has such a long arm behind it, doesn't reach over in places like the one where I was born and lift people out of humble and lowly stations and give them great jobs to do in life as an inspiration and an object lesson to other people to show what can be done when one recognizes the God-given power of thought and puts it to proper use.

We're living in a great nation and a great country. No matter what you might say about the administration in Washington, this one or any other administration; no matter what you may say about the government spending; no matter what you may say about the policies of this country in private or in government circles, this still is the finest country God has ever created and the finest there is in this world today.

You know, when I left Chicago in 1922, just after I had been editing and publishing *Napoleon Hill's Golden Rule Magazine*, all of my adversities and all of my opposition and all of my disappointments, practically, were experienced here in Chicago. And I said, "If I never see that town again, it will be much too soon." And, you know, there's a strange thing about making these very dramatic, definite statements: you better be careful what they are because they have a way of coming back and making you eat crow.

Of all of the places in the world I would never have chosen to have my business headquarters it would have been Chicago, and now I'm happy that I'm here because the opportunity of a lifetime was found only in Chicago. Someone has said that "God moves in a mysterious way his wonders to perform," and I never cease to think of that because I see it in operation every day of my life.

If I could have looked the world over and picked the man of my choice, the most suitable man in the world to help me to do the job that Mr. Stone is doing today, I couldn't have done better than I have done. And I didn't go looking for Mr. Stone at all; he came looking for me, which carries out the statement that he made while he was speaking—that when you are really ready, when you're ready for anything, by circuitous or direct routes it makes its appearance. If you're ready to make an association with me (association of student and teacher)—if you are really and truly ready—you'll find that tonight may mark one of the most important turning points of your entire life.

When I was conducting a large class out in Los Angeles some years ago, a man walked up to the stage to shake hands with me after the speech was over. He said, "Dr. Hill, I have every book that you've ever written. I think I've memorized most of them. I've underscored them. They have dog-ears on them I've used them so. And I want to ask you a question, which I hope you will not take to be too personal: If I should join your class, what will I get out of that class that I haven't already gotten out of your books?"

I want to tell you, that one stumped me for a moment. And then, as so often has happened to me and to my students at these moments of emergency when you're over the barrel, if you'll really and truly have assimilated this philosophy until you not only have it, but it has you, you'll know the answers. And in the flash of a second, the answer came, and I told him—I said, "Well, I'll tell you, sir, what you'll get out of the class that you will never get out of any of my books: you'll get a little hunk of Napoleon Hill, his enthusiasm and his faith. And I want to tell you that they're contagious." And he said, "That's just what I want, and I'm coming in."

And I would say to you, ladies and gentlemen, in closing my remarks, I would say to you that if you come into this class, I'm sure that you'll see the significance of my reply to that man, because if you'll really, truly tune in on the main-line of my source of faith and my source of enthusiasm, become indoctrinated with this philosophy, no matter what it is that you're doing in life, what it is that you want to do, you'll find the way always open. And I thank you very much.

Napoleon Hill put great emphasis in his writings and lecturing on the principle of *Going the Extra Mile*. Hill said this was the one principle that would get a person ahead faster than anything else one could do.

In nature, the law of increasing returns means the service we render with the right mental attitude not only brings back its true value, but is multiplied many times over.

—Don Green

Going the Extra Mile

Success Unlimited Speech

by
Napoleon Hill

Master of ceremonies, members of the club Success Unlimited, visitors, and friends of the radio audience, our lesson tonight is on the subject of *Going the Extra Mile*. And before I begin, I think I should define that term for you and tell you exactly what it means. "Going the extra mile," as it constitutes a part of this philosophy, means that you render more service and better service than you're paid to render, but you do it all the time and in a fine, friendly spirit.

Of course, you now know what it means. It means the thing that everybody is doing today—or does it? No, I hardly think so. I think perhaps one of the troubles of this old world today, one of the reasons for the state of chaos in which we find ourselves in this generation, is mainly that the majority of people not only do not go the second mile; bless your lives, they don't even go the first mile.

I don't believe there is a thing of principle in connection with this success philosophy that will get an individual ahead so far and so fast and so definitely as the habit of going the extra mile; that is, doing something useful for other people and forgetting for the time being about what you're going to get back in return. I would call your attention to the fact that the attitude in which you render this service is the important thing to be remembered.

When we went over this course before and I covered this subject, I promised you that I was going to tell you about the man who made twelve million dollars in return for sharpening two lead pencils. Would you like to hear me tell you about that now?

I think you will agree that twelve million dollars in return for sharpening a couple of lead pencils is quite a fancy deal, and it happened a good many years ago for a young man by the name of Carol Downs. He went to work in the office of William C. Durant, Mr. Durant being the man who organized General Motors. But at the time of which I speak, he was operating the Durant Motors.

Now, Mr. Downs was a young bank clerk in one of the big banks in New York City where Mr. Durant did business. And Mr. Durant went there one Saturday afternoon after banking hours, after the doors had been closed a few moments, to cash a check—a rather large check. And finding the doors closed, he took a coin out of his pocket and tapped on the window, and this young man Downs came to the door and opened it, saw who it was, and invited him in. And when he found out what Mr. Durant wanted, he said, "Well, we had closed the doors, but we haven't closed the vault. You can get the money." He not only cashed the check, not only did he open the door (he didn't have to do it), but he did it with a smile on his face and in a pleasant mental attitude that made an impression upon Mr. Durant. As Mr. Durant was leaving, he said, "By the way, would you mind coming over to my office next Wednesday morning? I'd like to have an interview with you."

Carol Downs went over, and Mr. Durant said, "I have been observing you over at the bank for quite some time. I notice that you are courteous. I notice that you go out of your way to do things for people and that you do it in a friendly attitude. And it just occurred to me that you would like a better opportunity than you have in the banking business. Perhaps you would like to come over here and get into the motor car business with me." Mr. Downs said, "Nothing would please me better, Mr. Durant, than to be associated with you because I have observed your operations for a long time. You're a big operator and a successful operator." They made a deal, and Mr. Downs went to work in the office of William C. Durant. They didn't mention any salary.

Staying the Extra Hour

The first day that he was there, when five o'clock came in the afternoon, they rang a large gong, and all of the people in that office—perhaps one hundred people—tried to get out of the office and onto the elevator at the same time. And out of self-defense, this young man Downs remained at his desk. After the people had all gone, he sat there pondering over what it was that caused the people working for such a grand person as Mr. Durant to want to run when the gong rang instead of walking out calmly. And while he was sitting there, Mr. Durant came out of his private office, saw this young man, and said, "Why, Mr. Downs, don't you know that we quit at five o'clock?"

Mr. Downs said, "Yes, Mr. Durant, I know that, but I was just sitting here pondering over the sight I've just seen." And then he repeated how these people had all made for the door. And finally, Mr. Downs said, "Mr. Durant, is there something I can do for you?" Mr. Durant said, "Yes, yes there is. I'd like to have a pencil. I'm looking for a pencil." This young man got up from his desk, went over to the stock room and got, not a pencil, but two pencils, took them over to the pencil sharpener and put two nice sharp points on them, walked over and handed them to Mr. Durant, turned to go away but he noticed that Mr. Durant was looking at him with unusual interest.

And something inside of him, some hunch, tipped him off that his sharpening those pencils and giving Mr. Durant two instead of one had attracted the attention of a great, outstanding businessman. And he made up his mind that thereafter, no matter how long Mr. Durant stayed after that gong rang, he would never leave that office until Mr. Durant had gone. He said, "I hoped that I would be in his way when he wanted something done, when he wanted another pencil or anything, and that he would have to call on me because there would be nobody else around."

Now, I want to ask you ladies and gentlemen, at that point, how many people have you known who would have stayed after the working hours were over just for the purpose of serving the man who was at the head of the business? How many people do you know who would have done that?

Later—Mr. Downs had been at this job about five months. They had fixed his salary; it was a modest salary—when one day Mr. Durant called him in and said, "Downs, we have just bought a new plant, an assembly plant over in New Jersey, where we're going to assemble automobiles, and I'd like to have you take this set of blueprints which shows where all of the machinery should be set up. Go over there and supervise the installation of the machinery because they're all going to be unloaded over there on Monday. Do you think you can do it?" Downs said, "I was foolish enough to tell him, 'Yes, I could.'" He took the blueprints and went out, went over into the park, and sat down on a park bench and looked at them, and he couldn't even read them. You know, bank clerks are not supposed to be familiar with engineering blueprints. But he did an unusual thing, ladies and gentlemen—an unusual thing such as the average person who isn't in the habit of going the extra mile would not have done: he said to himself, "Now, Mr. Durant is expecting me to do this job. I told him that I would do it. I can't do it, but I can find somebody who will and can." And he immediately got busy and employed an engineer at his own expense to go over there with him and help with the installation of that machinery.

Mr. Durant had told him that it would take him approx-imately three weeks. At the end of two weeks the job was done, and he reported back to the New York office. And as he went into the office, the telephone girl said, "Mr. Downs, Mr. Durant asked me to tell you to come into his private office before you went back to your desk." And when he got in there, Mr. Durant said,

"Well, Downs, you've lost your job while you were away."

"What? What, Mr. Durant? You mean, I've been fired?"

"Well," he said, "I wouldn't exactly put it that way, but I would say that you've lost your job. You can go back and clean out your desk."

Mr. Downs said, "Well, Mr. Durant, I thought I had done a pretty good job over there. I thought I had carried out my orders. I'd like to know for what I'm losing my job."

"Well," he said, "if you will notice that corner office, that private office down there as you go by, you'll find on the door of that office the name of your successor. Now, you go down and clean out your desk; get your personal belongings out."

And as Downs passed that office, he noticed on it "Carol Downs, General Manager." He rushed back to Mr. Durant's office and said, "What does this mean?" Durant said, "It means, sir, that you are now general manager and your sal-ary is fifty thousand dollars a year."

Imagine that—expecting to be fired and instead made general manager at fifty thousand dollars a year, not to men-tion Mr. Durant brought Mr. Downs into contact with the outstanding men of Wall Street through whom he got into the business of dealing in stocks and bonds. And in the succeeding five years, he made a net profit of twelve million dollars. And I can tell you that it dates back, ladies and gentlemen, to a circumstance so insignificant that the average person wouldn't have observed, wouldn't have noticed what was happening. It went back primarily to the time when this young man came out and opened the bank door when he didn't have to do it—when he admitted a man who wanted a check cashed and cashed it with pleasure with friendliness. I want to tell you that no matter what your business may be, no matter who you are or what your objective in life is, you'll never get very far in life until you form a habit of going the extra mile, of rendering useful service whenever and wherever you can possibly do it.

> *You'll never get very far in life until you form a habit of going the extra mile, of rendering useful service whenever and wherever you can possibly do it.*

Over forty years ago, I dropped out of Georgetown University Law School and had my first interview with Andrew Carnegie, the great steel master. And during the three days and nights that he kept me there, he sold me the idea of becoming the author of the world's first philosophy of individual achievement. And one of the conditions imposed upon me in return for his giving me this commission and influence and getting me the collaboration from successful men which I would need was that I would spend twenty years of my time in research without any subsidy from him, earning my own living as I went along.

When I went back to Georgetown University where my brother and I had matriculated and reported what had happened, my brother said, "Well, Napoleon, do you know that about all my life I have suspected you of being crazy, and from now on, I'm not any longer suspecting you; I *know* that you are crazy—absolutely crazy. Here you are, going to work for the man who has all of the money there is in this world, practically, for twenty years without compensation. Pray tell me, what are you going to use for money—oyster shells, I suppose?"

Ladies and gentlemen, I started with Andrew Carnegie in the fall of 1908. I completed my work in the fall of 1928, just twenty years from the time I started. True, I worked twenty years without direct compensation, but I want to give you a little outline of some of the things that have come out of that service I rendered during those twenty years.

To begin with, I have today, throughout the world, a following of approximately sixty-five million people who have bought my books, paid many millions of dollars for them. One book alone that I wrote, the book called *Think and Grow Rich*, has already grossed over three million dollars for the publisher and the editor—I mean the author and the publisher—and is destined to earn many more times that. I've turned out many more books under other titles that are selling in this and other nations. I have just recently completed another book, which I have now renamed *Success*

Unlimited, which I think will earn three or four times as much as *Think and Grow Rich*. And I would say the amount of money which my writings—due to my having gone the extra mile for twenty years—the amount of money that my books have earned up to the present time is more than five generations of my ancestors on both sides of the house earned during an entire lifetime. Now that's something to think about, isn't it?

When I started with Andrew Carnegie, I knew so little about the word *philosophy* that when I was through at his office, I went over to the library to look the word up. But during those twenty years of research, I learned a great deal about the word *philosophy*, and I have been able to produce a philosophy that has been so beneficial to men and women throughout the world that it has been estimated that if all of the successes I have helped to build through that philosophy—speaking now entirely of the monetary success, not to mention the spiritual and other successes which have come—if all the money earned by the people who have bought my books and have been guided by them were brought together, it would be sufficient to run the expenses of this government for at least, well, one hour, let us say. I think maybe you'll agree that that's a gross understatement of the facts.

I had lunch with my brother in Washington last summer. He took me down to a very good restaurant—the most expensive restaurant in Washington, something he had never done before. Previously he took me down to a cafeteria, where I generally paid for my lunch, and his too. I wondered what was coming up. He had a table reserved for Mrs. Hill and myself. He had a great, nice, large bunch of flowers on the table, and I thought, "Something's up. I don't know what it is, but I'll wait and see." And when we were seated, he arose and said, "I wish to make a speech. I wish to recall the statement I made in this very hotel some forty-odd years ago when I said that what you ought to do would be to go down to the psychopathic ward and have your head examined because I thought you were crazy for going to work for Andrew Carnegie for twenty years without pay." He said, "I now wish to reverse that statement, correct it, and edit it by telling you that the statement was correct; I addressed it to the wrong man. It was I who should have gone down to have my head examined," because he had done a little figuring and had found out that that one book I wrote, the book *Think and Grow Rich*, had earned more money than all of our ancestors probably had earned during an entire lifetime.

Now, there are many things I could have done in life, ladies and gentlemen, that would have been helpful to me in getting ahead. But I want to tell you, there isn't anything that I have ever accomplished, anything that I ever hope to accomplish, that hasn't been predicated very largely upon my willingness, my mental attitude, my spiritual attitude toward the subject of going the extra mile, and my willingness to apply and my habit of applying. I can recommend it to you as being the one principle that will get you ahead faster and quicker than anything that you could possibly do.

Quality, Quantity, Mental Attitude

I want to give you a formula. Perhaps you who are taking notes would like to take it down. I call it my "QQMA formula." And it means that "Q" plus "Q" plus "MA" equals the pay you receive in life, and the QQMA formula means the quality of the service you render, plus the quantity of the service you render, plus the mental attitude in which you render it, equals the pay you get out of life. And, ladies and gentlemen, when I speak of the pay, I don't have reference to that which comes in the pay envelope or that which is represented by bank balances. I'm speaking of the pay that comes in terms of the things that you need in this world—in the peace of mind, in the harmony and the understanding in the relationship that you have with yourself and with other people (the things that really count most in life).

One very outstanding thing about this principle of *Going the Extra Mile*—namely, you don't have to ask anybody for the privilege of adopting it. You can always act upon it. You may belong to some organization which looks with favor on your doing more work than you're paid to do, but if you wish to go it alone on your own individuality and you're willing to profit by men of the past who have succeeded, you will recognize that it pays for you to give the best that you have, no matter what you're doing; give it always, and give it in the right kind of a mental attitude. When you start doing that, you put behind you one of the great laws of nature. We call it "the law of increasing returns," whereby the service that you render not only brings you back its true value, but many times its value, and the pay that comes back to you oftentimes comes back from a different source from that to which you render the service.

The penalty, ladies and gentlemen, for not applying this principle—and you'll recall that all of nature's laws have both rewards and penalties—the penalty consists of the fact that if you don't apply this law, you'll bring down on you the law of diminishing returns. And the time will come when you not only will not be paid for as much as you're doing, but you will probably be kicked out of your job. I know of that happening too.

Now, I know well enough that there are some people in this world who believe that one of the troubles with them at the present time is that they're already doing more than they're paid to do. Well, if you're doing that, keep right on doing it—keep right on doing it, and then do a little publicizing of what you're doing. If you're working for an employer, for instance; you're rendering more service and better service than you're paid to render—slip a little anonymous note to his competitor and let him look you over for a while. It might do you a lot of good. Don't be foolish to go all the way through life rendering more service and better service than you're paid to render and not expecting that the world's going to recognize you, because if you do that, you'll wind up at a place called the county poorhouse. See to it that the world recognizes you.

One of the last things that Andrew Carnegie said to me after I had completed my work with him was, "I want you to go out into the world and not only teach this philosophy in the highways and byways of life, in every language on earth, if you can possibly get that opportunity, but I want you to demonstrate to all and sundry persons that you can make this philosophy work. And unless and until you demonstrate that you can make it serve you in causing life to pay off on your own terms, you will not have completed the mission to which I have assigned you." Ladies and gentlemen, those of you who know me intimately and well, as Bill Robinson, for instance, does, know that that time has come, that this philosophy has enabled me to make life pay off on my own terms and has brought me every conceivable thing that I need, or want, or desire, or can use. Of course I'd like to have fifty years added to my life, but I can get along on less.

Out in California there is a man by the name of Clifford Clinton who operates a series of cafeterias. And he told me that he and Mrs. Clinton went to Los Angeles ten years ago with ten thousand dollars in operating capital and a copy of *Think and Grow Rich* and started, then, in a little bit of a hole in the wall. And he said that—he was speaking to me about four years ago—and he said, "Today, my businesses are worth well over two million dollars, and I owe every dollar of it to your philosophy and especially to the unique plan under which I operate my cafeteria. And that plan is if a customer comes in and orders a meal and is not satisfied with it, as he goes out by the cashier, he can pay any amount that he wants to pay and nothing at all if he doesn't feel he's had his money's worth."

I said, "Well, Mr. Clinton, don't they take advantage of you now and then?"

"Well," he said, "perhaps a half-dozen times during a year we have somebody that tries to live off this cafeteria without paying."

And I said, "What do you do in that case?"

He said, "Well, we set a special table, we equip it with flowers, and we put a man at this table in uniform. And when that man comes in, we assign him to this special table. And after about three times doing that he gets tired of it and quits."

I said, "In other words, you kill him with kindness."

He said, "Exactly so."

I said, "What if he didn't take the hint?"

He said, "We'd keep right on feeding him, but we publicize it and have the newspaper men over there taking his picture."

Now there is a unique man who has gotten a hold of this one principle and has made it an outstanding success.

I'll tell you another experience. Out in a little town of Flagstaff, Arizona, which at the time of this circumstance that I'm now about to remind you of was nothing but a wide place in the road, there was an agent of the New York Life Insurance Company who was selling about enough life insurance to enable him to make a living, and all of a sudden, his sales began to go up so rapidly that the superintendent of agencies sent a man out there to see what had happened. And here is what had happened: This man had bought up a number of copies of *Think and Grow Rich*, had autographed them, and had written on the flyleaf in front of them, "This book has been of so much benefit to me that I want all of my neighbors and friends to have a chance to read it, and I am lending you this copy for one week. At the end of that time I will come back and pick it up and pass it on to some other neighbor," signed his name, and lo and behold, he found that when he went back to pick up those books, they generally invited him to come in and sit down; and he could talk about life insurance or anything else he wanted to talk about. Just that little gesture had brought the life insurance man and his prospective buyers together on a common plane of understanding and had torn down the resistance that people usually have against men and women who sell life insurance.

Life Insurance

You know, of course, that life insurance is one of the hardest things in the world to sell, and it really does have to be sold; nobody ever buys it. I found out about this incident when the New York Life Insurance Company made *Think and Grow Rich* a must for all of their salesmen and wired my publisher for five thousand copies of it at one time. Now that's a lot of books. Five thousand copies of a book is more than the average book in that field sells during its entire lifetime. All of this was predicated upon one man discovering how to make simple application of this marvelous principle of *Going the Extra Mile.*

When I was beginning to publish *Napoleon Hill's Golden Rule Magazine* right after World War I, I received a communication one day from a man by the name of Arthur Nash from Cincinnati, Ohio. Mr. Nash was a merchant tailor who wrote me a letter and said that he was in financial difficulties and would I please come up there and give him some counseling? I went to Cincinnati and spent several days with Mr. Nash, and we worked out a plan whereby he would save his bankrupt business by this principle of *Going the Extra Mile*. It seemed that a negative condition had crept into his business and all of his employees had suddenly become negative.

They'd slowed down in their work, business had dropped off, and there wasn't enough money in the treasury to take care of the payroll for the coming week. We worked out a plan. I submitted it to Mr. Nash. He called all of the employees together, and here is what he said to them: He said,

"Ladies and gentlemen, we've been working here together in this business for a great number of years. Some of you have been here as long as twenty-five years. And there was a time when this business was very profitable. We were making a lot of money. We had a lot of loyal customers all over the United States. And all of a sudden, the business has begun to slump, and it's gone downhill until we now are no longer able to make it pay. As a matter of fact, we're bankrupt. Napoleon Hill has offered a suggestion, which, I believe, if you will accept it and carry it out in the spirit it is offered, will save this business, it will save your jobs, and it will help everybody concerned.

"Now," he said, "I want to ask every one of you to come down Monday morning and start into your job in an entirely different spirit, an entirely different attitude—an attitude of friendliness, an attitude of willingness to go the extra mile and to put everything you've got into this job. If you'll do that and we can save the business, I'll not only pay you your back wages, but I'll pay you for the coming week, and at the end of the year we'll divide the profits up: part of them will go to me for the responsibility of running the business, and the rest of it will be divided equally among you. In other words, you will become practically partners in the business. I want you to know that this coming week, and perhaps the next week, you may not get any money at all. If you believe as I do that mental attitude, that confidence and faith can overcome a situation such as this, then let's all put our shoulders together and see what we can do." He had a lot of other things to say, but that was the sum and substance of his speech.

And he said, "Now, ladies and gentlemen, I don't want you to decide this moment. I'm going to leave the room. I'm going to stay away until you send for me. When you make up your minds whether you want to accept my proposition, send for me and I'll come in." He and I went to lunch. We were away about two hours, and when we got back, they said they were waiting to give their answer. And when we went in there, ladies and gentlemen, we found that these workers not only had agreed to accept these conditions, but they had gone home, some of them, and brought down their savings.

One woman had her savings in a glass fruit jar. I never saw so many nickels, and dimes, and pennies, and quarters, and half dollars in my life. They brought down their savings bankbooks, and they said, "Mr. Nash, we not only are going to accept your proposition, but we brought about three thousand dollars between us that we can put into the business right now. We're going to turn it over to you. And if the business earns it and can pay it back, all well and good, and if not, we will be willing to lose it because we made it down here with you."

They went to work on that basis, and as a result of that new attitude that sprang up between the employer and employees, the Arthur Nash merchant tailoring business became much more profitable than it ever had been in the early days of its existence. Now as far as I know now, although Mr. Nash has been dead perhaps ten years, he became very successful before his death. And as far as I now know, that business is still a prosperous, growing business because of the attitude of the people who worked there. I want to tell you that the time is coming—as a matter of fact, it's already here—when business and industry in general must get together with the employees and work out a similar attitude of going the extra mile—not only on the part of the employees, but on the part of the employers as well.

I have been instrumental in a great many cases throughout the United States in inducing management of industry to take employees into partnership with them on some sort of profit-sharing plan, and in every case, the industry doing that has made more money than it did previously. They have no labor troubles. They have written them an insurance policy against labor troubles. People are happier; they get along better. And if all the people would adopt and apply this principle of *Going the Extra Mile*, this would be a better world in which to live.

Now, when you adopt this principle of *Going the Extra Mile*, you will attract the attention—the *favorable* attention—of people who can and will (and often do) bring you vast opportunities, benefiting yourself in many ways that you'd never anticipated, just from going the extra mile. You know, nature is a wonderful power, and she makes it necessary for people to go the extra mile, especially those who have been chosen for great responsibilities in life. She tests them out in many ways. Now, I have a poem that I want to read to you that I think will bring to your attention one of the marvelous ways in which nature does this testing. I think that perhaps after I finish reading this poem, you'd like to have an autographed copy of it; and if so, I'm going to give it to you. If the radio audience wants a signed copy, if you'll write in for it, I'll see that it's sent to you. Here it is. It's by Angela Morgan, and it's entitled "When Nature Wants a Man":

> When Nature wants to drill a man
> And thrill a man,
> And skill a man;
> When Nature wants to mold a man
> To play the noblest part;
> When she yearns with all her heart
> To create so great and bold a man
> That all the world shall praise—
> Watch her method, watch her ways!
> How she ruthlessly perfects
> Whom she royally elects;

How she hammers him and she hurts him,
And with mighty blows converts him
Into trial shapes of clay which only
Nature understands—
While his tortured heart is crying and he lifts
Beseeching hands!—
How she bends, but never breaks,
When his goods she undertakes...
How she uses whom she chooses
And with every purpose fuses him,
By every art induces him
To try his splendor out—
Nature knows what she's about.
When Nature wants to take a man,
And shake a man,
And wake a man;
When Nature wants to make a man
To do the Future's will;
When she tries with all her skill
And she yearns with all her soul
To create him large and whole...
With what cunning she prepares him!
How she goads and never spares him,
How she whets him, and she frets him,
And in poverty begets him...
How she often disappoints
Whom she sacredly anoints,
With what wisdom she will hide him,
Never minding what betide him
Though his genius sob with slighting, and his
pride may not forget!
Bids him struggle harder yet.

Makes him lonely
So that only
God's high message shall reach him,
So that she may surely teach him
What the Hierarchy planned.
Though he may not understand
Gives him passions to command.
How remorselessly she spurs him
With terrific ardor stirs him
When she poignantly prefers him!
When Nature wants to name a man
And fame a man
And tame a man;
When Nature wants to shame a man
To do his heavenly best...
When she tries the highest test
That she reckoning may bring—
When she wants a god or king!
How she reigns him and restrains him
So his body scarce contains him
While she fires him
And inspires him!
Keeps him yearning, ever burning for a
tantalizing goal—
Lures and lacerates his soul.
Sets a challenge for his spirit,
Draws it higher when he's near it—
Makes a jungle, that he clear it;
Makes a desert that he fear it
And subdue it if he can—
So doth Nature make a man.
Then, to test his spirit's wrath

Hurls a mountain in his path—
Puts a bitter choice before him
And relentlessly stands o'er him.
"Climb, or perish!" so she says...
Watch her purpose, watch her ways!
Nature's plan is wondrous kind
Could we understand her mind...
Fools are they who call her blind.
When his feet are torn and bleeding
Yet his spirit mounts unheeding,
All his higher powers speeding,
Blazing newer paths and fine;
When the force that is divine
Leaps to challenge every failure
and his ardor still is sweet
And love and hope are burning
in the presence of defeat...
Lo, the crisis! Lo, the shout
That must call the leader out.
When the people need salvation
Doth he come to lead the nation...
Then doth Nature show her plan
When the world has found—a man![16]

Ladies and gentlemen, I think that one is very appropriate today. I think it's about time that a great leader comes to lead not only this nation, but the entire world. And when that leader does come—or maybe it will be more than one leader—but I say when those leaders come, you may be sure that they'll not be great unless they have been tested severely by adversity, by defeat, by setbacks, by disappointments, by heartaches, and you may be sure that they will never be great unless they come and inspire the willingness to go the extra mile on behalf of the people of the world.

Make it a Habit

Now, I want to give you some of the benefits that come from going the extra mile, from practicing it as a habit, from adopting it as your philosophy and using it from here on out. First of all, it places the law of increasing returns squarely back of you—and that's a marvelous thing. You know, this law of increasing returns is something to contend with. I read in one of the metropolitan papers the other day of an experiment that a farmer made out here in the state of Kansas involving the law of increasing returns as applied by nature. He took one thimbleful of wheat and planted it—just a thimbleful—and when that wheat had matured, he harvested it and planted the entire crop again; and then, he took the entire crop from that planting and harvested it and planted it again. He repeated that five times, and the harvesting, ladies and gentlemen, at the end of the fifth year of the planting was...guess how much? One hundred and sixty thousand dollars.

That's how prolific nature is when she starts paying off for doing the thing that you ought to do, for rendering useful service, for complying with her laws, for understanding them and adopting yourselves to them. And of all the laws nature observes not one is more inexorable than this law of going the extra mile, of rendering more service—I just said "planting more seed and better seed than you expected to plant."

Second, this habit brings one to the favorable attention of those who can and do provide opportunities for self-promotion. I don't know of anything in this world that would be so beneficial to a person working for a salary or for wages, or for another person, as to adopt this habit of going the extra mile, staying a little bit longer than is expected, not watching the clock.

That young man Downs, who worked for William C. Durant, had never heard of this principle of *Going the Extra Mile* when the circumstance I related first happened. Later on he became one of my most outstanding students. That's how I got his story.

And the last I heard of him he was still down in Atlanta, Georgia, going the extra mile, serving as counselor to the Southern Governors Association at the sum of one dollar per year. He said, "I have all the money I need. Now I'm getting a lot of satisfaction. I'm still going the extra mile." Now, as a result of that man's services, ladies and gentlemen, he has already brought to the South over five hundred million dollars' worth of industry. And the time is coming, it is believed by many who are capable of judging, that the South will transcend the North entirely in the business of industry, largely as a result of this one man's attitude of going the extra mile. There is no end to what will happen when you get the spirit of this principle and start living by it, making it your own principle—not just believing in it, but living by it.

Third, it tends to permit one to become indispensable in many different human relationships and thereby enables one to command more than the average compensation.

I don't know, strictly speaking, whether anybody is ever indispensable or not, but certainly there are people in this world who seem to be indispensable. And if there is such a thing as indispensability to which you may attain, it certainly can be more easily attained by the habit of going the extra mile.

And fourth, it leads to mental growth and physical perfection in various forms of service, thereby developing better ability and skills in one's chosen vocation. I have never written a book in my life, I have never delivered a lecture in my life, that I didn't intend to do it very much better than anything I had done previously. Sometimes I don't attain that goal, but I try to do it. And in the extra effort that I put into trying to do my very best I undergo a certain amount of growth, and it's been through that sort of effort that I have placed myself in the position where I rate as the number one man in the entire world in my field today—going the extra mile, giving unstintingly.

And next, it protects one against the loss of employment, and places one in the position to choose his own job and working conditions, and attracts new self-promotion opportunities. It enables one to profit by the law of contrast because the majority of people are not doing that. That law of contrast is something to contend with. Look around you and you'll find very few people going the extra mile. And when you start doing that, you attract attention—sometimes the envious attention of people who don't like what you're doing. But don't you stop on that account. You go right on doing it.

And next, it leads to the development of a positive, pleasing mental attitude, which is among the more important traits of a pleasing personality. And it tends to develop a keen, alert imagination because it is a habit that keeps one continuously seeking new and more efficient ways of rendering useful service. I don't think that I have ever engaged in delivering a lecture or writing a book that I didn't learn something during that effort that I hadn't learned before. Incidentally, I learned something about public speaking here last week. I didn't know about it until I got your reports back on my speech. And a little later on this evening when we get to the public speaking period, I'm going to tell you what I learned. It might be beneficial to you—which reminds me to remind you that you never become so perfect or so good or so successful that you can't learn. As long as your mind is open, as long as you are willing to learn, as long as you remain green, you'll grow. But the moment you become ripe, the next step is to become rotten.

Going the extra mile tends to develop a keen, alert imagination. I want you to remember that: a keen, alert imagination—because you're constantly looking for new ways of rendering service. Also, it develops the important factor of personal initiative, without which no one may attain any position above mediocrity and without which no one may acquire economic freedom. If you don't develop the habit of personal initiative, or doing the thing that you ought to be doing without somebody telling you to do it or going along with you to see that you do it, you'll never get very far in life.

Make it a Pleasure

Now, this business of going the extra mile and making it your business to take pleasure out of going the extra mile certainly does develop personal initiative. It causes you to get joy out of acting on your own initiative. And incidentally, that's the one thing that nature intended that every human being should do. Nature gave you the unquestionable right of power over your own mind and expected that you would solve your problems and, to an extent, work out your earthly destiny by the operation of your mind, but it would depend always upon your use of personal initiative—something you've got to do for yourself; you can't assign it to somebody else. Of course, there are a lot of people in the world who depend upon others to do their thinking for them, but people who are willing to do that, they reject the greatest prerogative that's been given to them by the Creator—the right to act upon, and use, and direct, and control their own minds.

Personal initiative is the most outstanding trait of the typical successful American citizen, and this is a nation literally built upon personal initiative. If it had not been for the personal initiative of those fifty-six brave men who signed the most marvelous document ever known to man, the Declaration of Independence—if it had not been for their personal initiative in doing that, we wouldn't be free agents here tonight. We wouldn't be able to go about in America doing the things that we want to do, saying the things that we want to say, as we are able to do today. It's been the personal initiative of the great industrialists, the great railroad builders of this country, and the great financiers that has made this the richest and the most desirable country on the face of this earth and has given us the highest standard of living ever known to mankind.

Men of initiative, men who are willing to go on their own, take their losses, make their failures, enjoy their successes, and take the full responsibility for their acts—those are the kind of people who get ahead in this world, not those who are looking for public relief or somebody to take care of them in their old age. There is one institution I can recommend where you have absolute security. I don't think any of you would want to go there. That's the penitentiary. You can get in there very easily, and you don't need to worry: your troubles are over for the rest of your life. I prefer to meet life on my own terms, to meet the conditions as they are on my own initiative, and to trust my knowledge of these marvelous principles of nature to get me to where I want to go in life and to get me there with the least amount of resistance.

And next, going the extra mile definitely serves to develop self-reliance. I noticed when you graded me on my speaking the other night there were three factors that you emphasized more than all the others: first, you graded me "perfect" on enthusiasm; second, you graded me "perfect" on self-confidence; and third, you graded me "perfect" on poise. And practically every one of you did that. Now, where do you suppose I got that poise and that self-reliance and that enthusiasm? I got it, ladies and gentlemen, by putting into everything I do the best that I have in active physical effort, in mental effort, and in spiritual effort—giving the best that I have, expecting that the best would come back to me. And lo and behold, the time did come when not only the best came back to me, but everything that my mind could conceive that I wanted, or desired, or could use was available to me.

And next, going the extra mile serves also to build the confidence of others in one's integrity and general ability. I don't know of any one thing that will raise you in the minds of other people more than for them to observe, as you go about your duties in your professional life—your business, or your job, or your work, or whatever it may be—as you go about that responsibility, that you are giving the best that you've got; that you're not watching clocks; that you're not griping, you're not complaining; and that you're not expecting that the world owes you a living. I like the man who believes that the world owes him only one thing, and that is the privilege of giving to the world the finest that he has.

Our next going-the-extra-mile benefit is that it aids one in mastering the destructive habit of procrastination. I suppose you've heard of that word, haven't you? Old Man Procrastination, he's something like Old Man River: he just rolls on and on and on and don't say nothing, but, ladies and gentlemen, he does plenty.

And next, going the extra mile develops definiteness of purpose, without which one cannot hope for success in any undertaking.

And next, it gives one the right to ask for promotions and more pay in a salaried job or a wage job, and nothing else on the face of this earth gives one the right to ask for promotion or more pay. I've watched people down through the years who have applied for more money, and oftentimes the reason for their asking for it would be something like this: A man decided he wanted more money and went in to see the boss and said, "Boss, I'd like to have my wages, or my salary, raised." The boss will say, "Well, what predicates your request?" "Well, my wife's going to have a baby." And, well, the boss said, "I had nothing to do with that, you know. That's your responsibility." Or, "We have sickness in the family." Well, the boss had nothing to do with that either. But when you go in with a record and say, "Look here, boss. I have been putting in considerably more time at my job than anybody else on the works. I've been producing more.

"I've had a good influence on everybody around. I've been doing this in a fine mental attitude. And I was just wondering whether or not you would like to give me some measure of recognition before your competitor finds out about me," you may be sure that would get attention. You would get it quickly if in fact you had been going the extra mile and rendering more service than you'd been paid to render.

Take this principle home with you tonight, make it your own, write it up in letters, and then try and put it in every room in your house, where every time you can turn around, you can see it—this one sentence: *Render more service and better service than you're paid to render.* And sooner or later, you will be paid for more than you do. Thank you.

Appendix

"This Changing World" Article, Letters, Etc.

The following is a short bio of Napoleon Hill that was published in *Plain Talk* magazine:

> Napoleon Hill has achieved a unique position in American life by making an exact study of the principles which cause personal success or failure, from both the material and spiritual standpoints.
>
> Born in a one-room log cabin in the mountains of Southwest Virginia, he overcame poverty with the help of a loving stepmother. As a young magazine writer, he came into contact with Andrew Carnegie, who suggested that he organize a "science of success"

so others might be spared the trial-and-error method by which Carnegie rose from humble beginnings.

During twenty years of research, Hill interviewed more than five hundred highly successful persons in all fields of endeavor. This research was the basis for his books, *Think and Grow Rich, How to Raise Your Own Salary,* and a course entitled the Science of Success. He also is the founder of a monthly magazine, Success Unlimited, published by Godfrey-Stone International Publications.

Oftentimes Hill's speeches were reprinted in newspapers and magazines. The following speech by Hill appeared in print in *Plain Talk.* Each issue was about sixty pages long and sold for twenty-five cents. The purpose of the magazine was to alert readers of the dangers of Communism. It was a bold publication to say the least, covering such topics as the murder of Jewish Polish prisoners.

Plain Talk was founded by Isaac Don Levine who was born in Russia in 1892 and came to the United States in 1911. Levine became a newspaper writer and covered the Russian Revolution of 1917 for the New York Herald Tribune. In the 1920s he returned to Russia to cover the Civil War for the *Chicago Daily News.* Later Levine worked for Radio Free Europe in West Germany.

The articles that appeared in the 1940s were timely and very important and remain relevant today. The range of topics was broad, covering such subjects as Palestine, China, Soviet spies in the US government, Korea, and much more.

Plain Talk attracted writers from the US and foreign countries with conservative, libertarian, liberal, and socialist interests. The writers were among the most highly respected in their field. Besides Hill, who had become well known for his 1937 publication, *Think and Grow Rich*, among several other books, other writers included Margaret Mitchell, author of *Gone with the Wind;* Sir Bertrand Russell, a famous British philosopher, mathematician, and social activist; writer Ayn Rand, famous for the book *Atlas Shrugged,* which is still popular today; and Clare Boothe Luce, who was a member of the US Congress, ambassador to Italy, and writer for *Vanity Fair* and *Time* magazine.

The article "This Changing World" was a recounting of Hill's talk on faith. It was recently found behind the fireplace mantel in a house in Wise, Virginia, the town in which Hill grew up. The house, known as the "Willie Banner House," was being remodeled by owner Thomas Kennedy, a local businessman. Banner was a sister of Hill's stepmother. Mr. Kennedy was kind enough to donate Hill's article, which is printed here for you exactly as it appeared in *Plain Talk* magazine.

—Don Green

This Changing World

by
Napoleon Hill
for Plain Talk *Magazine*

I have just made a great discovery!

I have discovered that I possess riches of great value. These golden nuggets were borrowed from life, but I will divide them with you if you want to share of my fortune.

The strange feature of my fortune is that I can profit by it only by passing it on to others. You too will discover that you can benefit from it most by spending it freely.

I began unconsciously to accumulate this wealth when I entered the greatest college on earth—the college of adversity! During the "business depression" I took a postgraduate course in this college.

It was then that I uncovered my hidden fortune of fabulous proportions. I made the discovery one morning when notice came that my bank had closed its doors, possibly never again to be opened, for it was then that I began to take inventory of my unused assets.

Come with me while I describe what the inventory disclosed.

Let us begin with the most important item on the list: faith! When I looked into my own heart I discovered that, despite my financial loss, I had an abundance of faith in the Infinite Intelligence and in my fellow men.

Along with this discovery came another of equal importance—the discovery that faith can accomplish that which not all the money in the world can achieve. When I was possessed of all the money I needed, I had made the grievous error of believing money to be power. Now came the astounding revelation that money, without faith, is but so much inert metal, of itself possessed of no power whatsoever.

Realizing, perhaps for the first time in my life, the stupendous power of enduring faith, I checked myself very carefully to determine just how much of this form of riches I possessed. I began by taking a walk into the country. I wanted to get away from the crowd, away from the noise of the city, away from the disturbances of "civilization," so I could meditate and think.

On my journey I picked up an acorn and held it in the palm of my hand. I found it at the roots of a giant oak tree from which it had fallen. I judged the age of the tree to have been so great that it must have been a fair-sized tree when George Washington was a small boy.

As I stood there looking at that great tree and its small offspring that I held in my hand I realized that the tree had grown from a small acorn. I realized too that not all the men living on the earth could build a tree like that one.

I was conscious of the fact that some form of Intangible Intelligence had caused the acorn, from which the tree had sprung, to germinate and grow. I picked up a handful of black soil and covered the acorn with it. I now held in my hand the visible sum and substance out of which that magnificent tree had grown.

I could see and feel the soil and the acorn, but I could neither see nor feel the Intelligence which had created a great tree out of these simple substances. But I had faith that such Intelligence existed. Moreover, I knew it to be a degree of intelligence such as no living being possessed.

At the root of the giant oak I plucked a fern. Its leaves were beautifully designed—yes, designed—and I realized as I looked at the fern that it too was created by the same Intelligence that had produced the oak tree.

I continued my walk until I came to a running brook of clear, rippling water. I took a seat near the brook that I might rest and listen to its rhythmic music as it danced on its way back to the sea.

The experience brought back sweet memories of my youth, when I had played by the side of a similar brook. As I sat there listening to the music of that little stream I became conscious of an unseen being—an Intelligence that spoke to me from within and told me the enchanting story of water, and this is the story it told:

Water! Pure, cool, gurgling water. The same water that has been rendering service ever since this planet cooled off and became the home of man, beast and vegetation.

Water! Ah, what a story you could tell if you spoke man's language. You have quenched the thirst of endless millions of earthly wayfarers; you have fed the flowers; you have expanded into the steam and have turned the wheels of man's machinery, condensing and going back again into your original form. You have cleansed the sewers and have washed the pavements, returning to your source, there to purify yourself and start all over again.

When you move you travel in one direction only—toward the great oceans from whence you came. You are forever going and coming, but you seem always to be happy at your labor.

Water! Clean, pure, sparkling water! No matter how much dirty work you perform you cleanse yourself at the end of your labors. Imperishable water! You cannot be created nor can you be destroyed. You are akin to life. Without your benevolence no form of life could exist.

I had heard a great sermon, a sermon that yielded to me the secret of the music of the running brook. I had seen and felt, through that sermon, added evidence of that same Intelligence that created the great oak tree from a tiny acorn.

The shadows of the trees were becoming longer; the day was coming to an end. As the sun slowly lowered itself beyond the horizon I realized that it too had played a part in that marvelous sermon I had heard.

Romantic Affinity

Without the beneficent aid of the sun there could have been no conversion of the acorn into an oak tree. Without the sun's help the sparkling water of the flowing brook would have remained eternally imprisoned in the oceans and life on this earth could never have existed. These thoughts gave a beautiful climax to the sermon I had heard, thoughts of the romantic affinity existing between sun and the water beside which all other forms of romance seemed incomparable.

I picked up a small white pebble that had been neatly polished by the rippling water of the brook. As I held it in my hand I received from within another and a still more impressive sermon. The Intelligence that conveyed that sermon to my conscious mind seemed to say:

Behold, mortal, a miracle that you hold in your hand. I am only a tiny pebble of stone, yet I am, in reality, a small universe. I appear to be dead and motionless, but the appearance is deceiving. I am made of molecules. Inside my molecules are myriads of atoms. Inside the atoms are countless numbers of electrons that move at an inconceivable rate of speed. I am not a dead mass of stone. I am an organized group of units of ceaseless motion. I appear to be a solid, but the appearance is an illusion, for my electrons are separated from one another by a distance greater than their mass.

The thought conveyed by that climax was so illuminating, so accelerating, that it held me spellbound, for I knew that I held in my hand an infinitesimal portion of the energy that keeps the sun and the stars and the little earth on which we live in their respective places.

Meditation revealed to me the beautiful reality that there was law and order even in the small confines of the tiny pebble I held in my hand. I realized that within the mass of that tiny pebble, romance and reality were affinities. I realized too that within the small stone I held in my hand, fact transcended fancy.

Never before had I felt so keenly the significance of the evidence of law and order and purpose that are wrapped up in a tiny bit of stone. Never before had I felt myself so near the source of my faith in Infinite Intelligence. It was a beautiful experience out there in the midst of Mother Nature's family of trees and running brooks, where the very calmness bade my weary soul to be quiet and to look, feel, and listen while Infinite Intelligence unfolded to me the story of its reality.

For the moment I was in another world, a world that knew nothing of "business depressions," and bank failures, and struggle for existence, and competition between men. Never in all my life had I been so overwhelmingly conscious of the real evidence of Infinite Intelligence nor of the causes of my faith in it.

I lingered in this newly found paradise until the Evening Star began to twinkle; then reluctantly I retraced my footsteps back to the city, there to mingle once more with those who were driven by the inexorable rules of "civilization" in a mad scramble for existence.

I am now back in my study, with my books, but I am swept by a feeling of loneliness and a longing to be out there by the side of that friendly little brook where, but a few hours ago, I had bathed my soul in the soothing reality of Infinite Intelligence.

Yes, I know now that my faith in Infinite Intelligence is real and enduring. It is not a blind faith; it is a faith based upon close examination of the handiwork of this Intelligence. I had been looking for evidence of the source of my faith in the wrong direction, seeking it in the deeds of men.

I found it in a tiny acorn and a giant oak tree, in the leaflets of a humble fern and in the soil of the earth, in the friendly sun that warms the earth and gives motion to the waters, in a tiny pebble of stone and in the Evening Star, in the silence and the calm of the great outdoors.

I am moved to suggest that Infinite Intelligence reveals itself through the boisterousness of men's struggles in their mad rush to accumulate things material in nature.

My bank has collapsed, but I am still richer than most millionaires because I have faith, and with this I can accumulate other bank accounts and acquire whatever I may need to sustain myself in this maelstrom of activity known as "civilization." Nay, I am richer than most millionaires because I depend upon a source of power that reveals itself to me from within, while they turn for power and stimulation to the stock ticker.

My source of power is as free as the air I breathe. To avail myself of it at will I need only faith, and this I have in abundance. The whole world ought to know by this time that faith is the starting point of every constructive effort of mankind and that fear is the beginning of most of man's destructive efforts.

Faith

Faith permits one to approach within communicating distance of Infinite Intelligence (or God, if you prefer that name). Fear holds one at arm's length and makes communication impossible.

Faith creates an Abraham Lincoln; fear develops an Al Capone.

Faith evolves a great leader; fear creates a cringing follower.

Faith makes men honorable at trade; fear makes men dishonest and stealthy-minded.

Faith causes one to look for and to find the best there is in men; fear discovers only their shortcomings and deficiencies.

Faith unmistakably identifies itself through the look in one's eyes, the expression on one's face, the tone of one's voice, and the way one walks; fear identifies itself through the same avenues.

Faith attracts only that which is helpful and constructive; fear attracts only that which is destructive.

Right works through faith; wrong works through fear.

Anything that causes one to be afraid should have close examination.

Both faith and fear have a tendency to clothe themselves in physical realities, through the most practical and natural media available.

Faith constructs; fear tears down. The order never is reversed!

Faith and fear never fraternize. Both cannot occupy the mind at the same time. One or the other must, and always does, dominate.

Faith can lift an individual to great heights of achievement in any calling; fear can and does make achievement impossible in any calling.

Fear ushered in the worst panic the world has ever known; faith will usher it out again.

Faith is nature's alchemy with which she mixes and blends the spiritual with the physical and mental forces.

Fear will no more mix with spiritual force than will oil with water.

Faith is every man's privilege. When exercised, it removes most of the real and all of the imagined limitations with which man binds himself in his own mind.

The fact that most men of science are free from all forms of fear, while those who know but little or nothing of science and natural law are steeped in it, is most significant.

Napoleon's presence on the battlefield is said to have been worth that of ten thousand soldiers because he inspired those around him with the spirit of faith in their ability to gain victory in warfare. What a lesson this is for business and industrial leaders.

When you no longer have faith you may as well write "finish" across your record because you will be through, no matter who you are or what you may be undertaking.

"For verily I say unto you, if you have faith as a grain of a mustard seed, ye shall say unto this mountain, 'Remove hence to yonder place,' and it shall remove; and nothing shall be impossible unto you." The business depression has, without doubt, tried the very souls of millions of people, but these same millions have learned through their trials that success cannot be achieved through fear.

Perhaps you are one of the millions of people who have read Napoleon Hill's classic work, *Think and Grow Rich*. One of the first stories in the book appears under the heading "Three Feet from Gold." In these pages, Hill repeats a tale told to him by R. U. Darby because of how well it illustrates that "one of the most common causes of failure is the habit of quitting when one is overtaken by temporary defeat."

This story focuses on the experience of Darby and one of his uncles. Excited about the prospect of finding gold during the gold rush days, Darby's uncle went west to make his fortune. He found gold, but the need for machinery made him return to his home in Maryland to get money from friends and relatives.

The gold seemingly ran out, and Darby and his uncle decided to quit searching for gold and return to their home. They sold their stakes and machinery to a junkman, who then hired an engineer and located gold just three feet from where they had quit drilling.

When Darby returned to Maryland and went into the insurance business, he discovered that desire could be turned into gold. He used the realization that he had missed a fortune because he had stopped just three feet from gold as inspiration for his work, saying, "I stopped three feet from gold, but I will never stop because men say 'no' when I ask them to buy insurance."

Prior to the publication of *Think and Grow Rich* in 1937, Hill published *Napoleon Hill's Golden Rule Magazine* and *Napoleon Hill's Magazine* between 1919 and 1923. For many years, Hill had lectured in cities and towns across the United States. Once he started the magazines, he used them as venues to advertise his ability to lecture upon the success principles about which he had been studying and writing.

The following is a one-quarter page ad announcing that Hill was giving lectures in Baltimore, Maryland, over a five-day period. Note that the ad was sponsored by R. U. Darby and Associates and the date was February 15, 1933. Hill had become very much in demand due to his two magazines and his willingness to speak.

When the ad ran for the lecture in 1933, Hill had already published his eight-volume set called *The Law of Success*, which was released in 1928. The revenue from this series came in monthly and was several thousand dollars some months. Hill, who had always been fascinated by automobiles, bought himself a Rolls-Royce.

The following ad is one of many that advertised Hill's work and helped put him in demand as a public figure.

—DON GREEN

THE OBJECT OF THIS FREE LECTURE COURSE

•

THE world has just passed through three years of chaos which has tried the very souls of men and women. Some have had the courage to hold on and to hope for the sunrise of a brighter day. Some have fallen by the wayside deeply wounded.

Through one of those strange turns of the Wheel of Fate our organization came into contact, a few months ago, with Napoleon Hill, author of The Law of Success philosophy and President of the INTERNATIONAL SUCCESS UNIVERSITY, of Washington, D. C.

Mr. Hill brought to us a new spirit of FAITH, new courage and an entirely new conception of the stupendous values which have come out of the "depression." As the result of this unusual experience we retained Mr. Hill for the entire year of 1933, for the purpose of stimulating the members of our organization so they will be able to make this the greatest year of our entire experience.

We are not contented to accept the services of a man who is as useful to the world as Mr. Hill without sharing the values he has brought us with our neighbors in Baltimore. We feel that this entire City needs mental, spiritual and financial rejuvenation, and we know, from our own experience, that Mr. Hill is the man to provide it.

We are, therefore, casting ourselves for a true Golden Rule part by presenting to our neighbors, without money and without price, a free lecture course under Mr. Hill's direction. No matter who you are or what may be your problems, you are welcome to attend these lectures as our guest.

Neither Mr. Hill nor this organization has anything to sell you during these lectures. Come prepared to receive a new awakening. Bring other members of your family or your business associates with you and observe, as we have done here in our own organization, that something will take place in your mind which will give you a new outlook on life.

Mr. Hill has had a rich experience all through life. He talks in terms that the man of the street understands. He not only tells people what to do, but he shows them how to put his philosophy of achievement into instant practice.

He is the author of the world's first philosophy of individual achievement and he has a student following in practically every country on earth. He has the honor of having helped more men and women to find themselves than any other philosopher of this age. You will be impressed by his frankness and the practicability of the ideas he will pass on to you during this lecture course.

Set aside all other engagements and attend the opening night lecture, then judge for yourself the values available to you. We have been serving our friends in Baltimore for more than thirty years. We would not assume the responsibility of sponsoring any man unless we knew, beyond room for doubt, that he would reflect credit upon us. We feel it an honor to be privileged to sponsor Napoleon Hill.

At the end of this lecture course we will add to our organization any person, either man or woman, who assimilates enough of Mr. Hill's training to gain his endorsement. The position will be permanent and profitable.

R. U. DARBY and ASSOCIATES
Baltimore Trust Building

▼

Letters

The following is the letter from Congressman Jennings Randolph that would become the inspiration behind Napoleon Hill's great book *Think and Grow Rich*. Additional letters written by Congressman Randolph follow.

—DON GREEN

My dear Napoleon:

My service as a member of Congress having given me an insight into the problems of men and women, I am writing to offer a suggestion that may become helpful to thousands of worthy people.

With apologies, I must state that the suggestion, if acted upon, will mean several years of labor and responsibility for you, but I am enheartened to make the suggestion because I know your great love for rendering useful service.

In 1922, you delivered the commencement address at Salem College when I was a member of the graduating class. In that address, you planted in my mind an idea that has been responsible for the opportunity I now have to serve the people of my state and will be responsible, in a very large measure, for whatever success I may have in the future.

The suggestion I have in mind is that you put into a book the sum and substance of the address you delivered at Salem College and, in that way, give the people of America an opportunity to profit by your many years of experience and association with the men who, by their greatness, have made America the richest nation on earth.

I recall, as though it were yesterday, the marvelous description you gave of the method by which Henry Ford, with but little schooling, without a dollar, with no influential friends, rose to great heights. I made up my mind then, even before you had finished your speech, that I would make a place for myself, no matter how many difficulties I had to surmount.

Thousands of young people will finish their schooling this year and within the next few years. Every one of them will be seeking just such a message of practical encouragement as the one I received from you. They will want to know where to turn, what to do, to get started in life. You can tell them, because you have helped to solve the problems of so many, many people.

If there is any possible way that you can afford to render so great a service, may I offer the suggestion that you include with every book one of your Personal Analysis Charts in order that the purchaser of the book may have the benefit of a complete self-inventory, indicating, as you indicated to me years ago, exactly what is standing in the way of success.

Such a service as this—providing the readers of your book with a complete, unbiased picture of their faults and their virtues—would mean to them the difference between success and failure. The service would be priceless.

Millions of people are now facing the problem of staging a comeback because of the Depression, and I speak from personal experience when I say I know these earnest people would welcome the opportunity to tell you their problems and to receive your suggestions for the solution.

You know the problems of those who face the necessity of beginning all over again. There are thousands of people in America today who would like to know how they can convert ideas into money, people who must start at scratch, without finances, and recoup their losses. If anyone can help them, you can.

If you publish the book, I would like to own the first copy that comes from the press, personally autographed by you.

With best wishes, believe me,

Cordially yours,

Jennings Randolph

Letter to Napoleon Hill
from Jennings Randolph, 1934

My dear Napoleon:

I was much pleased to have an opportunity to talk with you for a little while in New York the other day, and, following up our discussion, let me say that there are, as you probably know, more than five hundred thousand boys from the ages of seventeen to twenty-eight concentrated in the CCC camps of America, there being some 2,400 of these camps.

These boys need the service you are so capable of rendering through your "law of success" philosophy, and I wish to cooperate with you in taking the service to them by the most direct and simple method available. I shall present you personally to Col. Fechner, director of the camps, and I am hopeful I can open the door and gain admission for you on any reasonable basis you may suggest that will give you direct contact with these boys.

My suggestion is based very largely on the inspiration I got from your address over twelve years ago while I was a student of Salem College, and on the practical use I have made of your philosophy in my work.

I do not have in mind the sale of your books to these boys but some less expensive plan that will give them all they can absorb and use of your philosophy at very little expense to themselves or to the government. I have done considerable speaking for these boys recently, and I feel I know what their needs are.

The government has no program of education that approaches, in practical value, your philosophy, and if these boys need anything, they need the sort of training you can give them. Also, they need the same practical inspiration that you gave me at a time when this added touch helped me.

Most cordially yours,

Jennings Randolph

Letter to Napoleon Hill
from Jennings Randolph, 1953

September 15, 1953

Mr. Napoleon Hill

1311 Ethel Street

Glendale, California

Dear Napoleon:

Congratulations on How to Raise Your Own Salary! This important volume, I believe, will be stimulating for tens of thousands of persons who can profit by your dynamic law of success philosophy.

Tennyson once said—"I am a part of all I have met." The crossing of our happy paths thirty-one years ago is truly an attestation of that truism. The idealism as set forth in your memorable commencement address at Salem College in 1922, and later embodied in seventeen fundamentals of the science of success in Think and Grow Rich, has certainly been "a part of all I have met."

Your well-outlined formula proves that the key of progress is not always held by minorities, but that deeply rooted success is attainable for everyone, provided individuals are willing to advance and are unafraid to be different and creative in their thinking! I've often thought that the men and women who do the most for themselves, and for others, are the ones who have learned to fall intelligently. They may stumble but they rise to their feet again!

In the partnership of 4,500 workers in Capital Airlines led by President J. H. Carmichael, it has been our purpose to raise our sights as well as our salaries. This follow-through spirit, which is the practicing of your concepts, finds the company carrying two-and-a-half million passengers this year with gross revenue of approximately forty-five million dollars.

Remembering always your challenge and guidance, I am.

Faithfully,

Jennings Randolph

Letter to Lester Park from Jennings Randolph

March 16, 1935

Mr. Lester Park
Producer of "Pictures with a Purpose"
New York City

My dear Mr. Park:

May I not be among the first of the public men here at Washington to congratulate you upon your plan to present Napoleon Hill to the people of America on the talking picture screen and through personal appearances.

I have known Mr. Hill for more than ten years. I first came under the influence of his famous philosophy of individual achievement when he delivered the commencement address at Salem College, where I was a member of the graduating class. I am happy to acknowledge that the lesson I learned from that one address aided me in achieving my lifelong desire to represent my state in Congress, where I am now serving my second term.

I congratulate every person who has an opportunity to receive personal instruction from this distinguished business philosopher, whose mission in life is to help people to master their difficulties instead of going down under them.

You also are to be congratulated upon your decision to give the public the benefit of Mr. Hill's personal services before you present him on the talking screen, because I am convinced there are millions of people who need the counsel, and the inspiration, and the practical help that he can give. I am happy to see you present Mr. Hill to the public at this time because he is a great admirer of President Roosevelt and I am sure he will be very helpful in interpreting for the people the New Deal program.

Very sincerely yours,

Jennings Randolph

Letter to David from Blair, Sons of Napoleon Hill

David was the youngest of Napoleon Hill's three boys (he is also the father of Dr. J.B. Hill who proudly serves as a trustee on the Napoleon Hill Foundation Board). David spent his career in the military, serving in World War II and the Korean War. He became one of West Virginia's most decorated soldiers. He was also the last of Hill's sons to die. David was buried with full military honors at Arlington.

March 20, 1938

Dear David,

I have often wondered, since I left Lumberport the last time, how you were getting along and what you were doing. I have hoped so often to receive a letter from you.

I hope you are well, and likewise Jimmy and Grace and Judith. Do you play with the baby? I think Judith is so sweet and loveable!

Friday evening I had a letter from Mother. She told me she was worried about you and what you were planning to do now that you are not going to school. She also told me she thought Uncle Hood had told (or was going to do so) Aunt Mary to tell Jimmy he could put you to work for the gas company.

Now, I don't know how much credence is to be put in this bit of news. It may be so, or may not. But regardless, there are some questions that you should yourself resolve if you are ever to forge ahead in the future. I'm sure you will not mind if I take the liberty of discussing some of them in this letter, will you? For you surely know that no one else in the family, nor among your friends, can have a more personal interest in your future success and well-being.

From what I recall, evidently the age (and perhaps scholastic) requirements preclude your getting on with the Aviation Corps as you had desired to do when I was last home in February. If there were any chance of your getting on, I would be heartily in favor of it.

Barring that, your only other feasible resort at the moment is to go to work—possibly for the gas company, if Uncle Hood is willing to grant you the privilege.

I say "privilege" because I mean just that! You must remember, Uncle Hood could run the gas company with less actual help than he has now. I have often known that he and Uncle Vance were carrying more men than they needed but did so because they felt an obligation to help as many of their men as possible.

You remember the various times I have wanted to work for the company when I needed work and was put off because there was no work I could do until some was made up for me to perform? I imagine the same situation will exist in your case. It would be different if you were a skilled laborer such as a driller, driller's helper, welder, etc. But to be frank, you cannot do anything unless you have a boss over you (even as I had to have). You might get to dig ditches, perhaps work on the truck, or something similar.

But whatever you are put to doing (if you are lucky enough to get a job), let me urge you above all to stick at it! Chances are you will be put to work digging ditches. That is the cruelest, most backbreaking, most monotonous form of drudgery I know. Eight hours day after day, week after week, will make you so sick and tired it will seem like torture to continue at it. That is what I want to warn you about. If you are put at it, then for heaven's sake, stick with it regardless! No matter how tiresome, how grinding, how sick it may make you, don't give up. Stick with it without even a suspicion of a complaint on your part to anyone, and work well and honestly.

2.

When I say "well and honestly," I mean to really give value received for money paid, and then value plus besides. The reason? Simply because I know from experience (sad, at times) that Uncle Hood is far from being a fool! If he puts you to work, you may count on it—it will be for a purpose. Now you are nineteen, and almost twenty. You are no longer a boy. You're a full-grown man now (which is why I'm talking man to man with you on these pages). You might have been overlooked for getting drunk, for getting kicked out of school, even for all the black marks chalked up against your conduct in the past, on the grounds that you were still a youth, not old enough to begin to take life seriously. But all that has passed. People regard you now as a grown-up, a young man, who is strictly on his own.

Performance is what you will now be judged on, with your advent to maturity.

I know Uncle Hood well enough by now to know that underneath his hardboiled shell, his veneer of cynicism, his outward appearance of a man who is puritanical in that he tolerates no foolishness—underneath it all is a doggone swell fellow, a regular guy who cuts up plenty when he has a youth, a man who really does like all his nephews because they are his nearest of kin. David, there is nothing better that man underneath Uncle Hood's veneer would like than to see you make good and show that now that you've become a man, you can settle down and accept responsibility and make good!

You have an advantage over me in working for the gas company. I was never allowed to do more than to dig ditches with the gang or to work on the truck because these were the only places I could work without danger of getting hurt or killed because of my subnormal hearing. But you have normal hearing. You can go just as far as Jimmy—if you first show Uncle Hood you are willing and responsible.

The upshot of the foregoing, then, is, concentrate on the work you are given to do, and do it well. If you work with any of the other men, don't loaf any time you happen to see any of the others "resting." Keep at your work steadily. It is surprising, indeed, the number of unseen lieutenants Uncle Hood has always had who let him know when I was really "putting out" and just loafing.

If you work in the gang, don't let any of the men get you into any foolishness. If they make wisecracks, laugh at them, but keep your temper and go about your business. Don't ever take advantage of Pete by slacking on the job.

You'll find Pete to be your best friend if you get together with him by yourself at times and ask him if he thinks you are working satisfactorily and if he has any suggestions as to how you can improve. For the most part, though, if you yourself are <u>conscientious</u> in your work, I know your best will be more than satisfactory.

If any of the men ever play any jokes on you (practical jokes), take it good-naturedly, laugh at it, and go about your business. If you find out who did it, get them alone (regardless of who it is), and tell them you have no time for fooling around and if they do it anymore you're going to hang a mattock handle around over their head! Then tell them you have nothing against them so long as they don't play any more jokes on you—but that this is the first and last warning!

3.

Remember, if you get to work, Uncle Hood will have his eyes on you all the time! You'll have to admit that your past record hasn't been so hot. But it isn't your past that counts so much, David, but what <u>you do now and in the future</u>. So work hard, work steadily, and make your record entitle you to better and more pleasant jobs!

For eight or nine years I dug ditches before I got to work regularly on the truck. Jimmy had to dig ditches too before he got to walk lines, read meters, work on wells, etc., leading up to his present job in the office. You'll have always a "pull" in the higher-ups, David, but part of that "pull" will have to be hefty pulling you do of your own accord—at your bootstraps, if you get what I mean! And I think you do!

So much for your work at the gas company.

Self-Discipline

Now there are a couple other things I'd like to point out to you, David. First of all, if you really want to succeed, you have got to get yourself some self-discipline! To get to that point, while you are working for the gas company, you must renounce all pleasures of evenings during the week. Why? Because they keep you up late at night and sap your energy so that the next morning it is literally hell to crawl out of bed at daybreak to do work. Further, you will feel so tired you will hate the prospect of backbreaking labor. You will even be tempted to "feel sick" so you can take the day off. But common sense tells you, on the other hand, that if you are in bed and asleep every night by 9:30 or 10:00, you're going to feel rested, full of pep and energy the next morning—ready to tackle a hard day's work with zest.

Weekends? That's another story. You're entitled to let off a little steam on Friday and Saturday nights (provided you don't have to work Saturdays). Have your good times then, and you'll appreciate them much more. But don't overdo it—save some of your energy to do good work.

Liquor? You've had some pretty sad experiences with ole Demon Rum, haven't you? Mr. John Barleycorn seems to have taken you for a ride on several occasions, as you probably can remember if you think back. Now, I have no objection, personally, to liquor when used as an adjunct in sparing portion to enliven a dance, or before a football or basketball game, or when the "gang" gets together at the frat house for a reunion!

But David, at home in Lumberport that is a totally different story. No one has a right to get "pickled" anytime (unless they have decided to "end it all," when it doesn't matter) for reasons of health, to say nothing of the opportunity it gives a lot of small-town big mouths—a chance to gossip and ruin a mother's happiness because of the talk about her son! I'm not going to tell you to drink or not to drink. That is up to you. I drank myself once in a while, but anymore I seldom touch it. Just use a little discretion as to where you drink, be careful with whom you drink, and try to drink less than you think is enough. Of course it would be fine if you wouldn't drink anymore at all. But I wouldn't ask you to observe a rule that I didn't abide by. Anyway, you have as much brains, if not more, than I in deciding what's what when it comes to liquor!

4.

As to the kind of friends to have: Dave, I realize you don't have much to choose from in Lumberport. As a matter of plain fact, I honestly don't believe there is a single boy or young man up to your class in Lumberport. Most of the fellows are nice enough, but they don't amount to a tinker's dam! Most of them are lazy, without ambition to get ahead, like to go out and get drunk and run around with girls—not so much their fault, though, because they've been brought up in a poor environment, have never known anything different from what they have always had.

Dave, it is very true that "Birds of a feather flock together," and "Water always reaches its own level," and so on. Now, someday, if you work hard, you can be somebody! When you do, you won't exactly be proud to be known as cronies and bosom friends of town loafers, will you?

Don't misunderstand me, David. Far be it from me to strike any "holier-than-thou" attitude, nor do I want you to think I am turning snobbish. You know me better than that. I do like to be honest. Nevertheless, you might think this over too, along with all the other pills of wisdom I have been administering! For I sincerely believe you have too much potentiality in you to amount to something worthwhile to waste a lot of time in the evenings loafing down the street with small-town hicks or amateur Romeos.

What I'd like to see you do is to get in with the "right" crowd up in Clarksburg. Mix with the youngsters with whom Mary Virginia and Elizabeth Ann associate, and with the group that Jimmy and Grace know so well in Clarksburg. Best way to get started: Tell Jimmy you'd like to associate with the "right" crowd in Clarksburg. He'll get you started on the right track. Go to dances with them, out to the country club, etc., and let them introduce you around. Let people know your name is David Hornor Hill, brother of Jimmy Hill.

Budgeting Your Income

Now comes the biggest dose of this sermon—budgeting your income. Do you remember how Uncle Vance used to try to impress on Jack and me the value of a dollar? Chances are you'll be put to work, to start, at twenty-five cents an hour (same as Jimmy and I got when we first began) digging ditches. You're going to respect the sum of twenty-five cents like you never did before when you hold a quarter in your hand and say to yourself: "Golly, I earned this quarter! But how doggone hard it came! For a whole hour I had to lift a mattock up and down, shovel like hell, raise these blisters and callouses on my hands, and straighten up with a kink in the small of my back that darn near felt like it was broken! All this "chain-gang" labor for a quarter! But I earned it myself! Yessir!!!"

Then, David, you'll understand why, and what Uncle Vance meant, when he tried to make Jack and me appreciate just actually what a quarter represented. Every time I spent fifteen cents for a pack of cigarettes I almost cringed, and thought to myself: "Golly, this is thirty-six minutes of ditch-digging I'm spending!"

5.

The whole point is this: that money will come awfully hard. Naturally, I realize you'll appreciate it enough that you won't want to intentionally squander it. But we all know intentions don't mean a darn thing except they be followed through with appropriate action. What I'd like to suggest here is that you allot yourself so much money for spending money: tobacco, toilet articles, shoes, haircuts, for an occasional movie or dance once in a while. Allot yourself a total of between $1.50 to $2.00 a week. The rest put in the savings bank at Shinnston where you can't touch it. Save it so you'll have something to pay your own way if you ever decide you can really settle down to going back to school. See how long it takes you to save five hundred dollars. Then you'll have something for emergencies, for anything worthwhile in the future for which you will require a backlog of financial support. And David, you'll be surprised how much genuine self-respect the process of saving will give you!

Well, I figure I've done enough preaching here. I've tried to be constructive in the foregoing, David, and I want you to understand I've said these things only because I know they will certainly help you if you can remember them and follow through on them.

Please give Jimmy and Grace my love, and tell Grace to kiss the baby for Uncle Blair. With all my love to you, David, plus a printed (or typed) verbal handshake and good wishes that you have luck in getting to work, I'll close for the time being. Please write always.

Your brother,

Blair

P.S. David, if you have any spare time, please drop down and see Vera. She is going to move our things and live in the little house at the corner of the lawn of our home where Stones used to live. See if you can help her with carrying any of the heavy stuff. Find out what furniture she wants moved (she'll tell you) and then ask Pete Shreves or Clark Robinson to help you load it on their truck and move it, or carry it inside the little building, etc. Thanks a lot, David! BH

Endnotes

1. Warren Hilton, *Applications of Psychology to the Problems of Personal and Business Efficiency*, vol. 9 (New York: The Applied Psychology Press, 1920), 33-50. (Endnote added to original work.)

2. Ibid., 59-72. (Endnote added to original work.)

3. Wallace D. Wattles, *The Science of Getting Rich* (Holyoke, MA: Elizabeth Towne, 1910), 117-118. (Endnote added to original work.)

4. C. A. Munn, "Education and Success" in *The Fra Magazine: For Philistines and Roycrofters* 15 (1915), 144. (Endnote added to original work.)

5. This had to be in 1902 when Hill was about nineteen years old. Apparently, he worked briefly as a coal miner before attending business college.

6. The idea of performing more service and better service than paid for later became the principle *Going the Extra Mile*.

7. This was during the time that Hill worked for Rufus Ayers.

8. Hill apparently is making implicit reference to the importance of a willingness to take action.

9. This shows Hill's early thinking about the positive effects of failure.

10. Hill felt that "drifting" was one of the greatest reasons for failure in life.

11. Hill's first job in Chicago was as advertising manager for LaSalle.

12. The candy recipes had been passed down from Hill's mother, Sara Blair. His first wife, Florence, was skilled in making these candies.

13. Per Hill's biography, *Lifetime of Riches*, these cities were Chicago, Baltimore, Indianapolis, Milwaukee, and Cleveland.

14. The law of compensation may be "just rewards"!

15. This school was called the George Washington Institute of Advertising.

16. Angela Morgan, "When Nature Wants a Man," in *Forward, March!* (New York: John Lane, 1918), 92-95.

If you enjoyed this book, check out the full collection of
OFFICIAL PUBLICATIONS OF
THE NAPOLEON HILL FOUNDATION
BOOKS, EBOOKS, AND AUDIOBOOKS

The Power of Making Miracles

Napoleon Hill's Keys to Personal Achievement

A Treasury of Success Unlimited

Napoleon Hill's Greatest Speeches

W. Clement Stone's Believe and Achieve

Success With People

Napoleon Hill's Power of Positive Action

Napoleon Hill's Gold Standard

Wisdom for Winners Vol. 1

Wisdom for Winners Vol. 2

W. Clement Stone's Success System that Never Fails

Also available in print, ebook, and audio everywhere books are sold

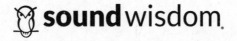

To claim your additional free resources please visit **soundwisdom.com/naphill**